I AM
BOUND AND
DETERMINED:

The Must Read Guide for Women

of Childhood Abuse and Trauma

Deidre Hughey

www.deidrehughey.com

Jasten Publishing – Apex, NC

Editorial assistance by Alice Osborn - http://aliceosborn.com/
Cover design by Spotlight Design -
http://www.spotlightdesignandphoto.com/

FIRST EDITION

Library of Congress Cataloging-in-Publication Data has been applied for.

ISBN-10 0-9827190-0-0
ISBN-13 9780982719008

ATTN: QUANTITY DISCOUNTS ARE AVAILABLE TO YOUR COMPANY, EDUCATIONAL INSTITUTION OR WOMEN'S GROUP
for selling, education purposes, subscription incentives,
gifts or fundraising campaigns.

For more information, please contact the publisher at
Jasten Publishing, 2306 Walden Creek Drive, Apex, North Carolina, 27523
919/924-3675—sales@jastenpublishing.com

Praise for I AM Bound and Determined:

"Practical, Uplifting, Sensitive and Mind-Enhancing"

As you turn the pages of Deidre Hughey's book, **I AM Bound and Determined**, you'll feel that doors are being opened. She writes about life possibilities in a way that allows you to truly feel their presence, and likelihood. Specific, practical, uplifting, sensitive and mind-enhancing. This book will change many women's lives.

Mary Jones, Host of The Mary Jones Show
WDRC, WSNG, WMMW, WWCO and NBC Connecticut
www.maryjonesshow.com

"It Will Alter Your Life"

When you are ready to see your destiny change, to be the Captain of your Life, give yourself an hour or two to read Deidre Hughey's **I AM Bound and Determined**, an inspirational book of resilient life stories, including her own, that will have you weeping, raging and cheering for every victory and happiness found and won.

If you are fortunate enough to pick up this "gem" of a book, I can guarantee that it will alter your life, change your thinking or give you the courage to try something new.

Frankie Picasso, Master Coach Trainer, Author, and Radio Host
Author of **Midlife Mojo**
www.unstoppablefrankiepicasso.com

"A Light That Encourages Us to Grow"

It is in sharing our stories that we help each other heal. Deidre Hughey has compiled compelling stories to show that there is light at the end of a dark tunnel, a light that encourages us to grow and become strong human beings despite the tragedies of our pasts.

Barbara Bentley, Featured on Dateline NBC and Lifetime Television
Author of **A Dance With the Devil**
www.adancewiththedevil.com

"A Wonderful Gift"

Deidre Hughey has given a wonderful gift to women of childhood abuse and trauma. Sometimes just hearing the honest stories of others is what it takes to realize that you're not alone. In the moment and in the years that follow trauma, it can seem as if there is no hope and no way to move forward. **I AM Bound and Determined** lets us know that there is hope. The wonderful women who have shared their stories and themselves in this book are real heroes. Perhaps their gift will allow other women to see just what is possible.

Ann Quasman, Host of WomanTalk Live
680 WCBM Baltimore
www.WomanTalkLive.com

"Order This Book Immediately"

Deidre's ability to take a subject like childhood violence and abuse, give women the tools to change their lives AND make them laugh along the way is truly her gift! If you are Bound and Determined to push aside your limits, embrace your true self & realize your dreams, order this book immediately! It will change your life!

Gwen Orwiler
Discover Your Dharma
www.discoveryourdharma.com

"A Chorus for Women"

Deidre Hughey does a great service by enlisting other survivors of abuse to share their stories of courage, hope and success. The reader hears from many with a common theme and that creates a chorus for women who suffer to realize that they are not only not alone but that together we can collectively heal and pass our stories of inspiration to others.

Patricia Raskin, Media Broadcaster and Award Winning Radio Producer
Author of **Success, Your Dream and You**
and **Pathfinding: Seven Principles for Positive Living**
www.patriciaraskin.com

"Insightful Book"

On page 99 of Deidre Hughey's inspiring book, **I AM Bound and Determined**, you will find these words: "You are not alone and there is hope for a wonderful future for you." Over and over again, through real stories lived by real women, this simple, sincere statement is reflected in every single account.

C. Leslie Charles, Author, Speaker, Trainer and Facilitator
Author of 6 books, including **Bless Your Stress**
and **Why Is Everyone So Cranky?**
www.lesliecharles.com

"Unforgettable Gift"

Reading **I AM Bound and Determined** was like viewing my own life through the eyes of the women featured. I related so closely with their trials and traumas and I literally cried because—for the first time in my life—I did not feel alone with my past. The courage, the determination and the grace with which these women overcame their pasts was so inspiring and motivating; they offered me permission to rise above mine. This book would make an unforgettable gift for any woman who has faced or is facing challenges in her life.

From trauma to triumph, from setback to survival and ultimate success, this insightful book will encourage you to review where you've been, how far you've come, and how to take the next steps in freeing yourself from old hurt that can hold you back and keep you from getting what you want and deserve in life.

CJ Scarlet, Founder of Roving Coach International
Author of **Neptune's Gift: Discovering Your Inner Ocean**
www.rovingcoach.com

"A New Perspective"

Deidre provides a testament to the healing and empowerment of women and their trials and tribulations. **I AM Bound and Determined** allows us to see that we all have our story and we all have the choice how we write the remaining chapters of our lives living with a new perspective. Leaving the victim role forever in the past!

Robin Marvel, Author and Speaker
Author of **Awakening Consciousness**
www.marvelousempowerment.com

"Inspiring"

I so enjoyed reading **I AM Bound and Determined**! It was fascinating and inspiring to hear the women's stories of trauma and their success beyond the pain. Life seems so crazy, chaotic and scary sometimes, as if we are all on a runaway train. **I AM Bound and Determined** helps to remind me to keep going and courageously take the next step in creating the life I dream of.

Susan Stanhope
Move Elders With Ease
www.MoveEldersWithEase.com

"A Circle of Friendship"

I AM Bound and Determined affirms that you are not alone and warmly invites you into a circle of friendship where strong character is a reflection of not only what you have achieved, but the obstacles you have overcome. By the choices these women have made, you too will be empowered to no longer be a slave to your past, but rather the director of your destiny. **I AM Bound and Determined** is also like good medicine that goes down like candy. It encourages us to not just change, but to transform by letting go and mastering the art of forgiveness which is the great human liberator.

Edie Raether, Speaker, Author and Coach
Author of 11 Books, including **Winning! How Winners Think - What Champions Do**
and **I Believe I Can Fly**
www.wingsforwishes.com

"A Bright Reminder"

I was deeply moved by the way she (Deidre Hughey) has allowed us (the readers) to connect to the authentic voice of each woman individually as their stories unfold like a compelling documentary. The sharing of these courageous women is a bright reminder of the resilience of the soul. Their ability to acknowledge and receive joy into their lives is an example for all of us to embrace the present for all it's worth.

Schelli Whitehouse, Speaker and Coach
Founder of The Next Highest Version of You
www.thenexthighestversionofyou.com

"Hopeful and Joyful"

Unlike many other books on childhood abuse, this does not teach you how to "recover" from your past. It shows you how to blow past it, and move into a future that is more hopeful and joyful than anything you've ever dreamed.

Jackie Kelm, Author and Speaker
Author of **The Joy of Appreciative Living**
www.appreciativeliving.com

"Unforgettable"

I AM Bound and Determined is a magnificent account of the wounds that heal. It is inspiring, hopeful, courageous and, at times, quite innocent. While it can be hard to read, you can be sure it was harder to live. These determined, powerful, willing-to-heal women share their stories of pain, hardship, abandonment and unspeakable trauma. But that's not why this book excels — in their own words you will experience the ferocity with which they love, the strength with which they recover and the resilience with which they re-invent themselves — that is what makes this book unforgettable. If you are in need of healing, or know someone who is, then you simply must read **I AM Bound and Determined**.

Nancy D. Solomon, Author and Speaker
Author of **IMPACT! What Every Woman Needs to Know to Go From Invisible to Invincible**
www.nancydsolomon.com

"A Community of Voices"

The journey to find post-traumatic peace is a tough and lonely one. **I AM Bound and Determined** offers not only hope, but a community of voices so that any woman struggling with the past will feel comforted in the present and inspired to move toward a better future.

Michele Rosenthal, Author and Speaker
Author of **Before the World Intruded**
www.healmyptsd.com

Dedication

Dedicated first and foremost to my family without whose support this book would never have been completed.

To my mom: Who I truly believe did the best she could as a parent and continues to learn and grow.

To Rhonda Britten and Marilyn Shannon: Rhonda for helping to open my eyes to my purpose and to Marilyn for giving me the strength and courage to have a voice.

To the five people that believed in me and whose love I felt as a child: Aunt Penny (my source of joy), Jan Benzing (aka "Mom"), Dr. Carole Hertz (my hero), Diane Williams ("My Bestest Friend") and Ora Cowgill (may she rest in blissful peace).

To the five women that helped me to grow as an adult into the person that I am today: Karen Machamer and Rubye Gillespie (two of the most wonderful women in the world), Carrie Kaibni (my dear sister), Susan Hughey (a woman of classic grace and was a part of my catalyst for change) and Debby Bruck (a gift from God).

To my son, Steven: Whose early battles and constant reminders of the fragility of life allowed me to become a better mother and love more than I thought possible. You are my ray of sunshine.

To my son, Jacob: Whose smiles, hugs, and laughter always bring joy to my heart. You are the rainbow in my life.

To my husband, Shawn: The love of my life...every day and for all days. You melted my heart of stone with your love, patience and understanding and for that, I will be forever grateful.

Thank You – I love you all.

TABLE OF CONTENTS

FOREWORD

"The Past is not your Potential, for Potential has no Bounds. Choose to break free from your self-imposed limits. Use your imagination to create a life of endless possibility. Experience your magnificence first hand..." **Unstoppable Frankie Picasso**

No matter how impossible you think this sounds, please listen up. No matter what you have experienced in your past or what you are experiencing right now, don't discount this yet.

Despite the emotional and physical abuse you have been subjected too, how depressed you are or sick and alone you feel in this moment, there is one truth you need to know. There is ALWAYS a "safe out" for you, a path that leads to your contentment and happiness. Yes, your life can improve dramatically, even exponentially but you need to be Bound and Determined to stick around and find out how!

When you are ready to see your destiny change, to be the Captain of your Life, give yourself an hour or two to read Deidre Hughey's " I AM Bound and Determined", an inspirational book of resilient life stories, including her own, that will have you weeping, raging and cheering for every victory and happiness found and won.

If you are fortunate enough to pick up this "gem" of a book, I can guarantee that it will alter your life, change your thinking or give you the courage to try something new.

All readers will be inspired by the tenacity and hopefulness that lives in the hearts of these heroines, and come to understand that there lives a common spark of determination and self preservation in each of us, should we decide to reach for it. All of these women found their own way to living contented, happy and successful lives despite their circumstances and beginnings.

I think the strength of this book is in the fact it's not about talking heads or people telling you what to do or how to live your life. What you do find, is real women baring their souls and reliving their traumatic lives so others can learn from them. Courageous women who willingly share their feelings, their pain and their private Hell!

Is it helpful to know that others have experienced the same pain, anxiety, emotional abuse? You betcha! Is it helpful to know that you can make your way back from the ABYSS and live a happy life? HELL YA! Life is an inside job, and this is where the healing and the living happens.

Unstoppable Frankie Picasso
Master Coach Trainer, Author, Midlife Mojo, Radio Host
www.unstoppablefrankiepicasso.com

~~~

It is always an honor to be invited to write the forward for another author, especially those authors who inspire, enlighten and transform the lives of others. One of my favorite quotes personifies the message in *I AM Bound and Determined:* Life is not about surviving the storm, but learning how to dance in the rain.

The courage and bravery of these successful women warriors gives hope to each of us overwhelmed with life's challenges. As each woman shared how she reclaimed her "self" and took back her power, hope is restored and permission is given to each of us to overcome our own personal struggles as well.

As we seek to define that common denominator in those who refuse defeat and always rise to their own greatness, we discover a positive and powerful belief system that fuels a personal passion and dog headed determination to not die with the music in us, but to sing our song. Our uniqueness is in how we sing it whether it be a thunderous roar or a gentle whisper in one's ear. While the styles and melodies may vary, what is consistent is the attitude that the show must go on!

By the choices these women have made, you too will be empowered to no longer be a slave to your past, but rather the director of your destiny. *I AM Bound and Determined* is also like good medicine that goes down like candy. It encourages us to not just change, but to transform by letting go and mastering the art of forgiveness which is the great human liberator.

I AM Bound and Determined affirms that you are not alone and warmly invites you into a circle of friendship where strong character is a reflection of not only what you have achieved, but the obstacles you have overcome. After all, an obstacle is something that you see only when you take your eyes off the goal. You must never lose sight of your vision. You must always dwell in possibilities, for how can the dream come true if you haven't first dreamed the dream?

Edie Raether, MS, CSP
Speaker - Author - Coach
Creator - Wings for Wishes

INTRODUCTION

The ache for home lives in all of us,
the safe place where we can go as we are
and not be questioned.
Maya Angelou

Have you experienced trials in your life?
Of course, we all have.

But this book isn't about trials, this book is about trauma.

Fortunately, we don't all have to experience trauma. But for those of us that do, the effects are devastating.

Webster's New World Dictionary defines **trauma** as:
1. a bodily injury or shock
2. an emotional shock, often having a lasting effect on the mind

---

Trauma can make you doubt everything you believe in. It strips your innocence, strips all feelings of security, and steals your ability to feel joy.

After all, what is there to be happy about? Your understanding of the world in which you live in and your place in it has been altered beyond recognition. And, that's not even the worst part.

So, what's the worst part?

No one understands.

Trauma takes away your hope and leaves you believing that your life will never, ever be better than the hell that you are currently living.

You feel alone.

You Are NOT Alone.

I know, because I've been there. I was sure that no one could possibly understand what I was going through...what I was feeling. I was sure that no one could make my pain go away. At the height of my trauma, I believed that the only way to end the hell that I felt was to kill myself.

That was 26 years ago.

Now, at the age of 42, I have a life that I never imagined was possible! I'm married to a wonderful man who adores me and I adore. I have two beautiful children. I have my own business, I write a column for a magazine and I'm a professional speaker.

Oh! And my 2 a.m. friends! They're incredible!! (Okay, that may sound a little confusing, but a 2 a.m. friend is someone that you could call at 2 a.m. and know that they would not only wake up and listen to you, but they would leave their house in the middle of the night if you asked. And, you would do the same for them.)

But none of that would matter if I didn't feel differently inside than what I used to feel.

So, how do I feel?

I feel that I deserve all of it and more. I love being loved and I love being able to love. And this is all possible because I feel safe and whole.

It took time for me to get to where I am today.

I was in therapy for years. I read self-help books, was in more therapy, read more books, went back to therapy, read more books, prayed, and read more books. But in looking back over my life and the number of years that it's taken for me to get to where I am today, I can honestly say that fighting for my life was worth every moment.

Why?

Because with as much intensity as I used to experience extreme sadness and emptiness, I now experience extreme joy and happiness! I wake up every morning looking forward to my day!

Why This Book and Why Now?
That's a great question.

As successful as I had become, there was still something missing. It wasn't debilitating by any means, but it was a feeling that there was more – I just couldn't put my finger on what the "more" was.

In October of 2008, I went to an event called Speaking of Women's Health in Raleigh, NC. There were 1,200 women in attendance from all over the state that had come together for this amazing event. There were health screenings, breakout sessions and three keynote speakers.

It was an awesome day!

Just before the third keynote I was talking with a group of people when we decided we really needed to get next door for the final keynote speaker. As we left, I noticed that one of the people in our group was going in a different direction.

I really didn't think much of it until that person walked out on stage! It turns out that I had been talking with Rhonda Britten, our final keynote for the day.

She was incredibly engaging and I was really enjoying her presentation. Then Rhonda became serious and began sharing her story about how her father killed her mother and then killed himself while Rhonda watched in terror. Instantly, 1,200 women became so attentive and quiet, you could have heard a pin drop.

At that moment, I realized what I had to do to make my life complete. I knew what was missing. I realized that my story was just as powerful as Rhonda's and could make a difference in people's lives. I had to find the courage within myself, just as Rhonda did, to get up in front of people and tell my story because my story could give women hope.

The basis for this book began out of the idea that my story, the story of my life, might be able to help someone else to have hope for their life where they may have none.

So, how did so many women get involved in this book?

As I began to write the book, the thought occurred to me that while my story would be able to inspire a certain number of people, it would miss others because I may not tell the story the way they need to hear it.

I knew that I was the only one who could tell my story. But I was certain there were others who felt like me and the book would be a much more powerful message of hope, if there were more people contributing.

I immediately thought of utilizing the service HARO (helpareporter.com) and I sent the following message:

> *My book is about women overcoming and succeeding. I'm looking for women who experienced personal trauma growing up (abuse, neglect, rape, etc.) but are now living their dream or beyond what they ever imagined! If this is you, and you're open to sharing what you have learned along the way, please send me your contact information and I will send you a questionnaire. PLEASE put "Book for Women" in the subject line of your email – deidrehughey@thebuzzbuilder.com*

I was hoping that I would get at least 10 people to respond to the request.

I was stunned as the requests for the questionnaire kept entering my inbox. Within the first 24 hours, I had heard from over 40 women who thought they fit the description.

To get to the heart of what each woman had experienced in their childhood, the questions were designed to be thought-provoking and somewhat invasive. I asked each woman to examine their past and share some painful memories.

The Questions

1. Why are you choosing to participate in this book?
2. As a child, did you have a dream about the future?
3. What is the trauma that you have overcome?

4. Why was this experience debilitating for you?

5. If you haven't already, please try to explain your thoughts and hopes about the future as you were experiencing your personal trauma.

6. What or who is it that helped you to overcome and move in the direction of healing?

7. What is it about your life right now that is different than you or others expected? (Please share your feelings and thoughts as well as the "what.")

8. If you had the chance to talk to a woman in the throes of what you experienced, what advice would you give her?

9. What is it that you are most grateful for in your life right now?

10. Do you have a favorite quote(s)? If so, would you please share it (them)?

11. Do you have a personal mantra? If so, would you please share it?

12. If you had a magic wand and could alter any part of your past, would you do it? Why or why not?

13. Is there a question that I have not asked that you think I should be asking you?

14. Is there anything else you would like to share?

I knew that I wouldn't get all of the questionnaires back. They were questions that were difficult for me to answer...and they're my questions!

In the end, I sent out 62 questionnaires and received 35 completed questionnaires in return. But I still didn't have permission to use the stories. I purposely didn't send release forms with the questionnaires. I wanted to be absolutely sure that each woman would have the chance to reexamine what they had sent to me over a period of time, to be sure that they were truly okay with sharing their experiences.

Out of the 35 releases that I sent out, I received 24 signed releases.

This book contains their stories. Our stories.

My Hope for You

My hope is that if you are undergoing a trauma in your life or have recently experienced a trauma, this book will help you to find someone that you can relate to. I want you to know that you're not alone. Every woman in this book has experienced a trauma, yet each one not only survived, but became successful.

My ultimate hope for you is that you seek help. Look at the resources page and call someone. Find a way to fight; we're here to tell you that it's worth it.

You are worth fighting for.

You **are** worth fighting for.

You are **worth** fighting for.

You are worth fighting for!

Did you hear me?

Every single one of us wants you to get help. If our stories can move you to get help, then telling our stories has meaning.

Nothing would make us happier.

If you're reading this book and your trauma is in your past, but you're not living the life that you dreamed of or have forgotten how to dream, I hope that you find inspiration in this book.

Every one of us in this book has felt at some point that we didn't deserve success, happiness or love. We understand what that feels like. But we also know that it's not true. It's not true for us and it's not true for you. There are resources in this book for you, too! Read self-help books, join a local support group, or take some online courses. Find a way to dream again and get support for your journey. You can find success!

What Is Success Anyway?

Success comes in many different forms and you have to decide for yourself what success looks like in your life. What would have to happen in your life for you to believe that you are a success? For some it may mean owning a business, being a therapist or a doctor. For many more of you, it will be having the ability to feel happy every day.

The women in this book are just like you. No matter how successful we are or what we've accomplished, we started out with trauma that sought to destroy our lives.

But we were not destroyed.

This book is a testament to
the will to survive
the ability to overcome
the spirit of forgiveness

This book is dedicated to and honored by
all of the women it contains
all of the women it will touch
the power of hope

We have fought back and spent years healing. Some of us are still healing. But we've healed enough to give back. We've healed enough to know that we have a story that can help you.

We want to help you to dream again.

We want to help you to live.

She has a degree in wisdom that life has bestowed on her.
Richard Nelson Bolles

HOW TO READ THIS BOOK

Within the framework of this book, each woman's story has been divided with parts of each of their stories inserted into each chapter in order to drive different points home for you, the reader.

Most chapters are comprised of three sections: an introduction and explanation of the question(s), all of the women's answers to the questions, and the closing to the chapter.

I welcome you to read this book from start to finish; however, you may find that there is a particular woman that resonates with you. If you find that to be true, I encourage you to read the introduction to the chapter, find the woman's name that resonates with you, read her section, and follow that by reading the conclusion to the chapter.

My hope is that the women in this book help you to grow chapter by chapter and that you allow them to make a difference in your life.

You may notice that almost every entry referring to a contributor has the woman's full name for you to see. One of the women opted to include her first name only and one asked for an alias. Whether the women used their full names or opted for a variation does not diminish the fact that it took a lot of courage for each of these women to share their stories with me and ultimately with you.

You may find that in reading this book that some of the chapters overwhelm you. I understand...some of them overwhelmed me. The only reason I could read some of the stories was because I knew that every woman ended up in a place where they see themselves as successful.

If you find yourself getting overwhelmed, that's okay, put the book down, take some deep breaths, go for a walk and call a friend. But eventually pick the book up again because the stories all have happy endings.
You will also notice that each chapter begins with a page of quotes. I asked each woman to send me their favorite quotes...quotes that encouraged

them and gave them strength. As you end one chapter and begin another, may their quotes give you strength as well.

My hope is this book moves you to a better place in your life. My hope is that this book inspires you to find greatness in your life, a place of hope and happiness. Better yet, I pray that you will eventually come to find it in your heart to give back to someone else and give them hope.

Give hope and live well.

Deidre

CHAPTER 1: THE POWER IN SHARING

Why have these women chosen
to share their stories in this book?

The Power in Sharing

"In Lak'ech"
Mayan Translation: "I am another yourself."

"You can get everything in life that you want by helping other people get what they want."
Zig Ziglar

"Bit by bit... she had freed herself. Freeing yourself is one thing; claiming ownership of that freed self was another."
Toni Morrison

"The ultimate measure of a man is not where he stands in moments of comfort and convenience, but where he stands at times of challenge and controversy."
Dr. Martin Luther King, Jr.

"Far better is it to do mighty things, win glorious triumphs, even though checkered by failure, than it is to take rank with those poor spirits who neither enjoy much nor suffer much for they live in that gray twilight that knows not victory nor defeat."
Theodore Roosevelt

The Power in Sharing

I think it's important to start this book with the reasons why each woman decided to participate.

Most people would not dare voluntarily choose to share such intimate details about themselves with people they know. Most would be even more private with the unknown world. And yet, these women chose to share in this book.

But why?

What would drive them to share things that most would keep hidden and buried? What drove them to answer the call to share the horrendous truths about their lives with the public?

The question I asked them:

Why are you choosing to participate in this book?

Their answers are varied and I think you'll find that they each hold genuine, heartfelt responses. These women come from different places and from all walks of life.

Each woman's answer is a revealing of her soul and a beautiful contribution to the rest of this book.

The answers also show the variety of women that have chosen to participate in this project.

We're Educated:

Dr. Nancy Irwin: To set others free. So others can learn that they are not alone. That healing is possible. If we have healed, so can they.

As a therapist I have seen so many peoples' lives affected dramatically by trauma and the after affects that have stayed with them through a lifetime.

Melody Brooke: Having survived so much and learning so much about myself and the things we do in our heads with what has happened to us, I think it's very important for people to know they are not alone and that there is a way out of the aftermath.

Dr. Karen Sherman: Because I want others to know that they do not have to be a prisoner to their past – that even though they have had dreadful childhoods, they can have a life that is full of joy. I believe that only by my being willing to reveal "my story" others know that it really is a possibility!

Dr. Donna Thomas-Rodgers: I want to make a difference in the lives of people. I have endured numerous obstacles in my life and I have survived all of them. I am still standing strong in the midst of adversity. Based off of my background, statistically I should have only finished high school and I should have several children and a job paying minimum wage. I have a doctorate, a great career and a consulting company in the works. I am writing books and helping others. I have a story to tell to empower and inspire.

We're Successful Businesses Owners:

Pam Lontos: I am participating because of my own story of how I overcame severe depression and went from an overweight, suicidal, depressed housewife who slept 18 hours a day, to VP of Disney-owned Shamrock Broadcasting in just three years without any additional education. I then went on to become a professional motivational speaker and am now the owner of PR/PR, a public relations firm that works with speakers, authors and experts.

Dana Detrick: I was really motivated to participate because I think I am just now arriving at that place I was meant to, where I'm able to see how much it can help others. I'm not "stuck in my story" from the perspective of a victim, nor do I want to shy away from telling my story at all, to keep from tainting my image or business. The truth is, this is part of my journey, and if it can make a difference in one person's life, it will be worth it for me to share it.

We're Mothers:

Linda Norton: One of the things in life dearest to my heart is children. My own children are young adults now; both in college. As they're setting out a plan, and deciding what education (among other things) they need to "have a chance in the real world," I find myself saying the same things to each of them, only to have it fall on deaf ears. The truth of the matter is that neither degrees, pedigrees, nor anything else that the world considers essential to success is really necessary – it can all be described as "icing on the cake." With or without those things, it is possible to succeed.

Happiness turns me on. I want for others to be happy and fulfilled. My hope is to share a message of belief in oneself with others, and the ability to live life in a way that, upon one's death bed, will be a life that you can truly say was well lived.

We're Givers:

Patricia Alcivar: My goal in life has always been to inspire other women and help them see the beauty of having faith both in their higher power and themselves. In the process, I feel I would continue to heal myself and tell my story.

Trish Lay: It is always my hope to express myself in telling of my life experiences in a way that will help individuals feel they are not alone in the process we call LIFE.

Revvell Revati: Because women need to know there is a way out no matter the situation plus, every time I tell my story, new memories come up and I can now see past the pain and into the future.

Katie Custer (Chakra Girl): I am choosing to participate in this book because I believe my story will empower and inspire many women to finally give themselves permission to live the life of their dreams. Every woman is stronger than she thinks...sometimes she just needs to know she is not alone in her struggles. That way, she can feel safe as she regroups – emerging as a force of nature when she is ready.

Diane Lang: Because I'm just like you –a survivor of abuse and depression and want to make a HUGE difference for other women.

We're Matter of Fact:

Jillian Montes: I feel I have something to share with other women to possibly help or inspire them.

Dr. Glenda Clare: I am choosing to participate because I feel that it is time for me to talk about my experiences. I believe that by sharing, I can help others.

Diana De Rosa: Because my story seems to fit the type of person you are looking for.

Ungenita Prevost: I know I have a story that can inspire thousands.

Dr. Barnsley Brown: Because I have finally, in my speaking, been sharing my childhood story with POWER and I want to share it in writing as well!

We're Spiritual:

Cynthia MacGregor: If my story can help others, that will be a good thing. I have long believed in what I have always called "universal paybacks," a concept that has in more recent years become known as "paying it forward." This is one way for me to "repay the universe" for all the people who have helped me throughout my life.

Rev. Brenda Bartella Peterson: Because I, too, have lived a challenging life and have learn to move beyond the challenges and thrive. I applaud the notion that those of us who have learned to thrive are called to give back by sending the message of how we learned to others who long to know. I think thriving after trauma is very doable but it requires support on multiple levels.

My hope is that this book would provide readers with sources that could reach out to for support. It is, indeed, the traumatized who must make the choice to reach for the kind of support they need to heal. It may even take several attempts to find the right support for your particular needs.

We're Hopeful:

Jennifer: I would like to give young girls hope....Your current situation may be terrible but that doesn't mean your future has to be the same way.

"Sarah": It is my desire that perhaps something shared from overcoming my former trauma can help give another person hope. Hope that life has some amazing rewards that can be realized. It is possible to get across such an abyss and live a fulfilling life.

Shirley Cheng: I choose to participate in this book to bring hope and healing to your readers. Life is the most precious present God has bestowed upon each and every one of us, and I wanted people to realize and recognize the importance and blessing of life, of every minute, of every second. People need to know that obstacles do not stop you; you stop yourself.

We're All Sharing...

The women in this book have shared from their hearts. They have shared because their story can give another hope. They shared because they remember the pain. They shared because they hope they can make a difference. They shared so that their stories can give someone else a vision for the future.

They shared to give hope to you.

They shared to make sense of the senseless.

The Power in Sharing

Chapter 2: The Power and Danger of "Now"

"Now" has a power that is overlooked.

The Power and Danger of "Now"

There isn't anything I can't do.
Dr. Karen Sherman

The past is history. The future's a mystery. But "now" is a gift; that's why it's called the present.
Scott DeMoulin

What would you do if you knew you could not fail?
Author Unknown

If you believe in yourself then nothing is impossible.
Author Unknown

What you see depends on what you look for.
Author Unknown

The Power and Danger of "Now"

The Power and Danger of "Now"

What do you want to do when you grow up?

As a child, you were probably asked this question by a wide variety of people. Parents, siblings, aunts, uncles, teachers, clerks at the grocery store...perfect strangers felt the liberty to ask you what you wanted to be when you grew up. You probably asked this question of yourself. And depending on the circumstances and age you were asked, your answer probably changed.

> **Jillian Montes:** *I wanted to be a singer and a dancer.*

> **Dr. Glenda Clare:** *I wanted to be a medical doctor.*

> **Ungenita Prevost:** *I wanted to be a performer.*

> **"Sarah":** *I really wanted to be an astronaut or geologist.*

> **Cynthia MacGregor:** *I wanted to be a Broadway actress.*

Over the course of the years, here's how I would have answered that question:

Age
1 - 8: a veterinarian
9 -12: help people and make them laugh
13-15: no idea, but I'm going to go to college
15-17: future...is there a future?
18-20: future? I just want to get through college
21-25: heck if I know, I'm just trying to pay my bills
26-30: not be miserable
31-35: anything but what I'm doing now
36-38: help people
39-Now: help to move women of all ages to embrace their lives, disregard limits and realize their dreams...laughing along the way!

The Power and Danger of "Now"

As a child, a dream had a way of brightening our days with visions of what the future held. It was powerful to think about the future...it could drive us and excite us about what we were to become. We weren't thinking about **how** to achieve our dreams; we just knew that they were things that we wanted.

> **Shirley Cheng:** *I wanted to be the president of the United States.*

> **Jennifer:** *I dreamed I was going to be a lawyer because I was great at arguing.*

> **Dr. Barnsley Brown:** *I wanted to be a circus ringmaster, a sleuth like Nancy Drew, and a famous actress.*

> **Pam Lontos:** *As a child, I wanted to go into advertising.*

> **Diana De Rosa:** *I wanted to travel the world.*

It's interesting that over the course of the years, our focus tends to be less on the dreams of the future and more on the realities of what's happening "now."

"Now" has a particular power, because we are living it. We can see it, touch it, and feel it. It has a power because we are experiencing "now" on a daily basis. "Now" has a way of taking our attention off of our dreams. As the focus shifts from our dreams to what is happening in our daily lives, our dreams begin to lose their brilliance. The very dreams that spurred us onward begin to fade.

> **Melody Brooke:** *Only that I would find real love... oh, and that I would be a princess!*

> **Revvell Revati:** *I dreamed I would be driving down Sunset Boulevard in Hollywood, driving a convertible and/or surfing the waves on the beaches of California and Hawaii.*

> **Dr. Donna Thomas-Rodgers:** *I dreamt that I would be a famous lawyer.*

Dr. Karen Sherman: *I think I had the same dream as every other little girl; that is that I would get married and have a family and be happy. I also dreamt that my mother and I would get to have a relationship with each other.*

This fading of our dreams becomes more pronounced as we face disappointments. We grow weary from the negativity that we face in our lives. Between the media, friends, family and co-workers, our senses are assaulted with failures.

"You want more out of life? Get in line!"

"How do you think you're going to be able to do that?"

The first time we hear these things, they surprise us. They shake us to the core. Over time, we begin to accept that these words are true. We start to doubt that we can ever achieve our dreams. Once we begin to doubt, we stop thinking about our dreams, and we stop focusing on them. We grow even wearier when we don't achieve our goals.

The danger of "now" is that because of its power over our thoughts, it can become all we see – the danger of "now" is that it cripples our dreams and holds our creativity captive. In the end, "now" is the executioner of hope.

This becomes even more debilitating when we are put in circumstances beyond our control. As a child, trauma is out of our control. There's nowhere for us to turn, we can't defend ourselves and we get confused by our reality.

Trauma makes our dreams shift and have a different meaning than for children under "normal circumstances."

Dreams after or during trauma…
have a different meaning:

Patricia Alcivar: *As a child, dreaming about the future was what saved me and took me out of the horror I was living. I used to dream of being a beautiful and strong athlete and living in a beautiful house and waking up to the beautiful smell of the ocean and/or park. I dreamed of being admired and feeling special none of which was even remotely possible living at home.*

Dana Detrick: *My dreams for the future kept me going. I somehow knew in my heart that there was a different place for me, a different life, and I saw myself as being separate from my circumstances. It was just incredibly confusing, because the knowledge I didn't have was how I was going to get from point A to point B. But I did believe I would get there.*

Dreams after or during trauma…
get cut short:

Diane Lang: *I really don't remember that much – I repressed a lot BUT I do remember writing a kids' newspaper in Kindergarten and early elementary. I wanted to be a writer and even an activist.*

Dr. Nancy Irwin: *I wanted to be a singer…a performer…a speaker…a writer. Anything with words… I was not free to express my feelings as a child.*

Dreams after or during trauma…
aren't based in reality:

Trish Lay: *Being adopted, I had a fantasy my father was a Prince and my mother, a Princess. And one day they were going to find me and take me back to their castle on a white horse and we were going to live happily ever after. Other than this fantasy, I had no visions of my future.*

Dreams after or during trauma...
aren't the dreams of a child:

Linda Norton: *My only recurring hope was to raise children in such a way as to break the cycle of abuse that had apparently existed in my family for generations.*

Rev. Brenda Bartella Peterson: *As a child, my sole dream was to go to college...I thought college was my ticket out of poverty and our family craziness.*

In fact, some can't dream at all:

Katie Custer: *I do not recall feeling capable of dreaming of a "real" future.*

As children, we dream to shape our future.
Trauma steals our dreams.
Without dreams, we lose hope.

Without hope...

The Power and Danger of "Now"

Chapter 3: The Dream Destroyers

The traumas that stole all hope,
and in some cases...

the will to live.

The Dream Destroyers

Someone was hurt before you; wronged before you; hungry before you; frightened before you; humiliated before you; raped before you, yet someone survived.
Maya Angelou

I have learned not to judge a man by his success, but rather by the obstacles he has overcome while trying to succeed.
Booker T. Washington

Great spirits have always encountered violent opposition from mediocre minds.
Albert Einstein

The Dream Destroyers

Every woman quoted in this book has overcome tremendous traumas. Before delving too deeply into this chapter, it's important to note that some of the women's stories are horrific. In all cases, no child, **no human being** should have to overcome the obstacles put into the lives of these women.

These stories aren't here for comparison to your trauma or the trauma of a loved one. They aren't meant to be compared to each other.

Each person experiences a trauma from their own perspective, their own history.

Just because one trauma seems less severe than another on the surface doesn't give anyone the right to judge the effect that it may or may not have had on the bearer of the trauma.

Let me explain...

Our own experiences are our only personal benchmarks for the severity of life. If the very worst thing that happens to a child is that their parent spanked them, then for them, that experience is the benchmark for trauma in their own lives. They can feel that spanking with similar intensity as the child that is beaten, because it's their personal benchmark.

If you are the survivor of childhood trauma but haven't found your path to happiness or success...or perhaps, don't believe that it's possible, our hope is that you find yourself on these pages. Even if it's not the same experience, we hope that you will recognize the thoughts in these women's shared experiences.

We all hope that you do find yourself on these pages and then remember that every woman on these pages no longer sees themselves as a victim but as a survivor.

No. Each of them is more than a survivor. They are successful, beautiful women.

They are a celebration.

YOU are a celebration!!

~~~

"What is the trauma you have overcome?"

Tourette's; Agoraphobia; Severe Anxiety Attacks; Rejection

Cynthia MacGregor: In school, I was teased and imitated by the other kids, disciplined by some teachers (including a health teacher—a HEALTH teacher!!—who threatened to send me to the vice principal's office if I didn't "stop it." I got up and went to the nurse's office—I knew there was no way I could stop it—did he really think I would twitch and make noises like that if there were humanly any choice?), and generally made to feel bad.

On public transportation (both in my teens and in my adult years thereafter), people sitting next to me would get up and move to another seat to get away from me. My father, who died less than a year after the onset of my Tourette's, went to his grave believing I could have stopped it if I wanted to. And when my mother remained a widow for several years, my grandmother guilted me by opining that no man would want to marry a woman with a daughter who did what I did (twitch and make noises), and if I would just try harder to stop it, my poor mother could find herself another husband.

Meanwhile the anxiety attacks and agoraphobia grew worse, so that it was very difficult for me to leave the house at all.

In my senior year of HS, the situation grew intolerable and I dropped out of HS just a few months short of graduation.

But nonetheless at age 18, I moved to NYC where twitching, making noises, and freaking out as badly as ever, I still managed to live on my own and hold down a job, although people still edged away from me and there were still some days when I just couldn't leave the house (due to the agoraphobia).

Abandonment; Death of Parent; Foster Home

Ungenita Prevost: When I was about two years old my Father took me away from my mother. From the time I was two to 12 years old I was raised by a woman whom I thought was my biological mother. I always had issues with my identity and never felt totally connected. Later it was diagnosed as abandonment issues. From a very young age I would sabotage relationships. I never knew why I had so many difficulties connecting at school or life for that matter.

A few months before my 13th birthday, I was watching TV with the woman that I thought was my mother and she had a seizure right in front of me. I can vividly recall the terror and the ambulance coming to take her away. That was the last time I saw her.

Consequently, a month later I was introduced to my REAL MOTHER. What a roller coaster my life was. My stepmother died while I was being introduced to my biological mother. This is where most would think "Live Happily Ever After"…not. I had a tumultuous relationship with her and we bickered during my teen years which landed me in a Foster Home at 15.

At 17 I received my walking papers from Child Welfare Services. That's how I started my life. It was difficult, challenging but through those struggles I pushed forward. I had to learn to work through those things that were embedded deep within my self-conscious.

Dislocated Hip Socket

Diana De Rosa: I was born with a dislocated hip socket. From a year and four months old until I was three years old I was in and out of hospitals and had all different types of casts put on me. They weren't sure that I would ever be able to walk. I did walk but spent much of my life with a limp because one leg ended up shorter than the other.

Physical Abuse; Verbal Abuse; Emotional Abuse; Drugs

Dana Detrick: My mother is what I now realize to be a narcissistic sociopath. I believe drugs were a big part of her life, and that perhaps there was some dissociative problems going on below the surface too, due to her traumatic experiences as a child. This lead to physical, verbal, and emotional abuse predominantly on her part.

Emotional Abuse

Pam Lontos: I had a very negative upbringing dealing with emotional abuse and severe depression.

Poverty; Sexual Abuse; Physical Abuse; Loss

Rev. Brenda Bartella Peterson: As an adult---Burying two husbands and my son, Mark. As a child---Poverty, instability, molestation, physical abuse and dysfuntionality.

I went to 14 different elementary schools. I never lived in the same house two years in a row until I was 26 years old. My father was married 9 times (only six women but nine marriages). My mother was married four times. THREE of those marriages were to each other. They truly loved each other and had no skills for building a marriage.

I have been married five times. My first husband died of complications of MS from Agent Orange in Vietnam. My second husband died of lung cancer. My smart mouth comment about marriages three and four is, "When you have lived through what I lived through, get back to me about the mistakes you made and we will talk about the mistakes I made." Marriages three and four were nice men and big mistakes.

My fifth marriage has truly been a gift. John and I were married in Jan 2002 and my son, Mark, was killed in a tragic accident in April of that year. This marriage has been my salvation in the years that have followed. While we have lived through many difficult circumstances in seven years, the relationship itself has grown deeper and richer.

Sexual Abuse

Katie Custer (Chakra Girl): At age 31, I was learning energy work (Reiki), practicing "laying on of hands" on myself as a bedtime ritual, and had a memory of childhood surface. It was my first experience with flashbacks. Over the next two years of meditation, shamanic counseling, energy healing, and journaling, I uncovered a minimum of five incidents of childhood sexual abuse. These memories remain mostly repressed.

Neglect; Emotional Abuse

Diane Lang: Well, neglect (child abuse) and an eating disorder – anorexia from ages 10-18 and then again at 25 when my dad died.

Alcoholism; Physical Abuse; Verbal Abuse; Emotional Abuse

Dr. Barnsley Brown: I grew up in a cold, abusive family in which there was alcoholism, manic depression, physical violence, and sexual abuse. My response to all of this was to take it into my body in the form of severe allergies to foods, grasses, fur—a list of things over three pages long—and debilitating asthma that resulted in many hospitals visits and stays. At times I did not expect to live through my childhood.

Abandonment; Rejection

Trish Lay: The initial trauma of my life occurred at day one; being separated and disconnected from my Birthmother. The outcome from this trauma translated to learning how to deal with issues of abandonment, rejection, and extreme disengaging cellular loss.

Severe Juvenile Rheumatoid Arthritis; Debilitating Pain; Legal Injustice; Psychological Abuse; Physical Ailments (Loss of ability to walk and loss of eyesight)

Shirley Cheng: I have scaled quite a few high mountains and swum across quite a few deep oceans throughout my relatively short twenty-six years of existence. I was diagnosed with severe juvenile rheumatoid arthritis at only eleven months old, leading me to a mountain range I climb even to this date.

I spent my early years in constant pain; some days, I could not even sit up or move a muscle, and every slightest jolt would cut through me like knives. My beloved mother, Juliet Cheng, who is the God-sent light of my life, has saved my life numerous times from the grasp of death.

She took me to China six times in a span of ten years to seek treatment. Once, in China at age four, I was actually able to walk for one whole year receiving Western shots combined with massage therapy. For the first time, I could run and dance with the wind.

Unfortunately, my walking days soon ended when the quality of the shots went downhill after they were put on mass production. Of the times we lived in America, my mother and I fell victim to America's medical laws concerning children's medical care and parental rights. She lost custody of me twice only after refusing unwanted, harmful treatments that could have sent me to my grave, or worse, paralyze me.

The first case happened when I was twenty-two months old. Mother was told that if she lost the custody case, she would not be allowed to see me for twenty years. And the last case in 1990, when I was seven, made international headlines; my mother and her lawyer, George Athanson-- former mayor of Hartford, CT--appeared on CBS This Morning show with Paula Zahn. Fortunately, my mother won both cases, thus saving me from a fate worse than death.

I was too young to remember the first case, but for the second, I remember the horror and anger I felt when they suddenly pushed me away from my mother just as she found out she lost custody of me after being tricked by the doctor. Yet, I had deep faith in my mother. I just knew she would win. Win she did, but only after five long months fighting in courts and after I had become all skin and bones under the doctor's "care," which consisted of administering Naprosyn to me on an empty stomach, making me vomit a large amount of blood.

I believe that the custody cases were most traumatic in my life among all of my challenges. I was also mistreated by my one-on-one aides when I went to school. I had aides ranging from unloving to incompetent and everything in between. I complained to my school, they ignored my voice, and I kept on hurting, except during eighth grade when I had the most wonderful and caring principal.

I am always passionate about learning, and I thoroughly enjoyed going to school; but my unpleasant experiences with those who cared for my physical needs were always a hindrance to achieving complete happiness in school. I had aides who came to school very ill; and one was a heavy drinker who often fell asleep in class and one was a smoker who left me to go out to smoke. My last biggest challenge was the loss of my eyesight at age seventeen.

Rape; Abortion; Illness

Dr. Glenda Clare: I was raped during my sophomore year of college. I was 17 years old and a virgin. As a result of rape, I got pregnant. I had an abortion. Also a result of my rape, I got pelvic inflammatory disease. At the age of 18, I was faced with the knowledge that I would never have children.

Sexual Abuse; Physical Abuse; Psychological Abuse; Verbal Abuse

Patricia Alcivar: I wouldn't say that I have completely overcome my past and I honestly believe that no one completely overcomes their past. However, I do believe that people learn how to deal with their past challenges and not let them destroy their future. I was sexually and physically abused by my father from the time I was about 3 years old until 8 years old. He also gave me the worst beatings that literally scarred me for life. Then I was mentally and verbally abused by my mother from 8 years old until 15 years old.

Abandonment; Parental Divorce; Rape

Jillian Montes: I was date raped at the age of 15, did illegal drugs and went from man to man (co-dependent relationships). This all occurred after my father left and my parents divorced.

Sexual Abuse; Dyslexia

Melody Brooke: My father and my grandfather and an uncle sexually abused me – all before I was 5 - and then a neighbor when I was 6 and just starting school. I couldn't concentrate and was dyslexic on top of it. I was depressed and thought I was horrid and stupid.

Sexual Abuse; Emotional Abuse

Dr. Nancy Irwin: I was molested by our Presbyterian preacher. It began at age 14, and continued through about age 18. In those days, no one talked about these things, and of course he told me not to tell... "No one else could possibly understand what we have." I was already shut down from expressing my feelings at home anyway, and at least this guy took time to answer my natural questions about sex. I felt special, yet dirty, all at once.

Death of Parent; Gang-Rape; Physical Ailments

Revvell Revati: My father died when I was 12. At 13, I became suicidal; my mother, brother and I never got along. At 18, I left home. At 19, I was gang raped and kept with a well-known biker group for 2 weeks. By the time I was 33, I had asthma so bad I didn't see myself living to 40.

Psychological Abuse; Neglect; Verbal Abuse; Sexual Abuse; Physical Abuse

Dr. Karen Sherman: Being raised by parents who subjected me to every type of abuse there is. The neglect was the worst. I ended up growing up feeling awful about myself and constantly overcompensating or taking on behaviors that were not in my best interests.

Physical Abuse; Verbal Abuse; Psychological Abuse

"Sarah": I grew up in an abusive household with no love or emotional support, and was also beat up all the time in high school, which left me with absolutely no sense of self nor self-esteem. The story: My parents divorced when I was six, and my mom got custody of me and my sister.

Shortly after the divorce, my maternal grandfather passed away, so it made sense that my maternal grandmother moved in to help with our care while my mom went back to school to get a job.

My grandmother, I think, actually ended up resenting having to raise children for a second time, and took it out on my sister and me both physically and emotionally. We got a lot of overzealous beatings for relatively minor offenses, which accelerated when we hit our teens, when my grandmother began drinking in the afternoon and was well-oiled by the time we got home after school. She was always looking for someone to pick on by that time, with me usually as the target.

In fact, there was one time that I got beat up by the school female bully after school and came home bleeding with an almost-broken nose, and my grandmother did nothing. She said I deserved it without hearing the why and the how, and refused to even talk to me. I sat up in my room bleeding and crying for three hours before my mom got home and eventually took me to the emergency room.

My grandmother and I particularly did not mix well from the start. One time when I was seven years old, I had snuck into the laundry room as a hiding place, and accidentally overheard my grandmother tell my mom, "I hate her!" (referencing me). And I also remember specifically being told by my grandmother at another point when I was a young teenager, "You won't ever amount to a piece of shit."

I do want to be clear that my sister and I were squeaky clean kids. We read a lot. We made our beds. We were strictly regimented in every aspect of our lives including having to ask permission to ride our bikes around the block every single time, even if we wanted to go around more than once. We never smoked, drank, did drugs, skipped school, and were academic achievers (well, my sister more than me- that's why she was my grandmother's golden child).

My mom would then also conduct what I called "Spanish Inquisitions": This was where any shrugged or muttered answer to "How was your day at school?" was met with a stern order to come out into the living room, and for the next 2-4 hours, my personal life was slowly and painfully dissected until I didn't have a shred of self esteem left.

It's like my mom was trying to get into my very soul, and wouldn't let me have any private thoughts. Everything I did or thought was called into question and criticized in a very cold, calculated and almost clinical way. (My mom was a biology professor).

When finally released from those sessions, I would go upstairs to my room and cry for another hour – hollow and empty. Compounded with this sterile, harsh and abusive environment, my mom and grandmother had a warped sense of what it meant to be an individual. They were convinced that they needed to make us stand out as individuals by wearing home-made clothes, and therefore avoid conformity. That did not go over well in a small, conservative Wisconsin town (did I mention we had moved there from Louisiana, so I had an equally noticeable Southern accent and brown skin from being so tan?)

The result: I ended up without any self-esteem, looked and acted completely different and had the crap beaten out of me at school then again at home by a drunk and angry grandmother. My mom, as detached as she was, stayed away from the confrontations as best as she could, letting my grandmother rule the roost with her iron fist. My sister and I came up with the nickname "ICU" – Iron Claw Unit.

Fitting.

In my senior year, I attempted suicide by hanging myself in the clothes closet I shared with my sister. I was so far beyond in despair – my family didn't want me, and I couldn't fit in at school – the kids hated me too. At that moment, I felt that my life was worthless. My sister was in the room and I closed the door behind me. I tied up the scarf and hung it tight, then let go. I managed to get to the point that I had lost consciousness and was already seeing the "white light" – I heard a roaring noise, too. But at that moment, the wooden pole that the clothes were hanging on broke, and my sister heard the commotion and opened the door.

Then all hell broke loose.

My mom came storming up the stairs to see what the matter was. What happened became clear. She did nothing except berate me about my actions, grounded me, and considered the matter closed. Chagrined, I resigned myself to fate and continued to barely function, ashamed of my failed attempt. But fortunately, graduation came, and I escaped to college and out of that environment.

At that time, I started questioning my life and decided to re-contact my father in my attempt to find myself and who I was. When my mom found out about this through her post-high school Inquisitions, she became completely irate and the maddest I've ever seen her. She told me that I had betrayed her and everything she had worked so hard to accomplish.

Specifically, she thought she had finally covered her tracks so my dad would never find us, but I had "ruined it." Interestingly enough, she was going to school to become a counseling therapist, and had plenty of psychological arrows in her quiver – she completely threw the book at me and told me I had gone insane, and should look into institutionalization. And I believed her.

I was frantic that I had betrayed her (love) and lost everything important in my life. Fortunately, the university campus had a counselor on site, and if it wasn't for him providing the prevailing rational voice in my life, I probably would have had a second suicide attempt for sure.

Thank God it didn't come to that!

Alopecia (spot baldness)

Dr. Donna Thomas-Rodgers: I was diagnosed with Alopecia at the age of 19. I have spent almost 17 years covering up and then discovering who I have become because of my hair loss. I am missing 50 percent of my hair. I tried all types of medication and shots and it only caused me emotional and physical duress. I now wear wigs everyday and I feel good about who I am. I still struggle with the illness but I am stronger and more confident than I have ever been in my life. I now know that hair today can be gone tomorrow but who I am will last a lifetime.

Abandonment; Physical Abuse; Psychological Abuse; Emotional Abuse; Rape; Drug Trafficking

Jennifer: Where to start.....My parents separated when I was 5...I moved in with my mom and my dad moved away. My mom would tell me terrible things about my father because she was angry and wanted me to hate him.

I didn't see him for two years...My mom was heavily into narcotics and would leave myself and my brother locked in our room with no food for over 24 hours...

Other parents would have to drive me home from soccer practice when I was 6 because my mom would forget to pick me up. My father stepped in and took us to live with him when I was 8. Starting a new life, my brother and I were living pretty happily until my dad met his new girlfriend. I knew something was off about this lady but I couldn't figure it out...

About 6 months into their relationship she started beating my brother and me emotionally and physically. I soon found out they were both snorting speed and smoking weed. My father would say nothing as my new stepmom would send my brother and I on hour-long missions to look for Tupperware that wasn't there. Screaming at us when we told her it wasn't. We would come home from school to her being extremely angry. She would throw ashtrays, shoes, or whatever she could find at us. Telling us we were no good and belittling us in any way she could. If our room wasn't clean she would shove us into a corner and hit us with a belt.

As I started to get older I would stand up to her but that only resulted in fist fights. She would get on top of me and hold me down so I couldn't move...her son raped me and when I told them they didn't believe me. Drug traffic soon started to come in the house when I was about 13...I ran away at age 16 and never went back.

My father went to Prison for 2 years and my step mom went to jail for a year on drug charges and child endangerment. I moved in with my boyfriend's mother at the time, a nice Christian lady. I reunited with my mother 7 years later who came clean from drugs but is now dependent on bipolar medication.

I moved in with my boyfriend when I was 18 but became an alcoholic, drinking a half gallon of Jack Daniels daily. I worked as a CNA full time and went to school once a week. (I was expelled from high school for smoking marijuana.)

My boyfriend became possessive and started becoming physically and mentally abusive. I started doing cocaine everyday and lost my job. I decided it wasn't worth it anymore and took a handful of Valium. That didn't work out so well. After that day I moved to Orange County and started a new life...

Physical Abuse; Mental Abuse; Sexual Abuse

Linda Norton: Oh gosh... I'm not quite sure where to start. I was an abused child; physically, mentally, sexually... every possible way. I have zero education... I was "awake" during one math class and two typing classes in my 12 years of schooling. The rest of the time, I existed in a sort of semi-conscious state; most likely as a result of the extreme abuse I endured on a daily basis. The closest I can come to describing my own state of being during those first 17 years of life is by reminding you of the character that Sigourney Weaver played in the movie *Ghostbusters* when she was physically invaded by a foreign critter and literally suspended a foot over her bed, panting. That was my normal state for the first 17 years of life.

Mental Abuse; Emotional Abuse; Abandonment; Sexual Abuse

Deidre Hughey: I was under the distinct impression that my parents didn't want me. I was hospitalized in first grade for two weeks for pneumonia. In third grade, my family was building a house on a 15 acre lot. My parents decided that it was too much to take care of me while I was in school. They made arrangements with the local gas station owner (Ora and Major Cowgill) for me to bathe, eat and sleep at their house during the school week. I didn't understand why I couldn't stay with my parents and began a cycle of trying to get in their good favor to get back with my family.

A lot of my memories are still repressed. I do remember being so very glad that our family had dogs, because I knew that they loved me. They would wag their tails when I came home, lick my face and lie with me on the grass under the sun.

I was rarely hugged or told that I was loved. In fact, my sister and I began to hate it when our mother would come home because we knew that she would find something wrong with how we conducted our day.

At the age of 12, I was molested by a 19-year-old over an entire summer and threatened to be beaten to death if I told anyone about him. At one point, he held a 2x4 board over my head to show me how he would kill me as I cried and begged for my life.

At 13, a farmer in town hugged me and put his tongue in my mouth until I finally got away. Later that same year, one of my relatives (an uncle by marriage), fondled my breasts. After my first year in college, I was date raped...I became convinced that all men were the same and only wanted sex.

~~~

These stories are a celebration of the adversity that a person can overcome. All of the stories are full of heartache, most are full of despair. Many of us did not believe that we would survive, much less that we would ever live a happy life. And few, if any, ever thought that we would live successful lives.

We hope that if you've found yourself in this chapter that you don't stop reading. Recognizing that we are not alone is only the first step.

These are our stories.

But we're so much more...

The Dream Destroyers

Chapter 4: The Individual Effects of Trauma

Trauma affects each of us differently.

In some cases, the same trauma can cause one soul to choose death, while another chooses life.

It is not the critic who counts, not the man who points out how the strong man stumbled or where the doer of deeds could have done better. The credit belongs to the man who is actually in the arena, whose face is marred by dust, and sweat, and blood; who strives valiantly, who errs and comes short again and again; who knows the great enthusiasms, the great devotions and spends himself in a worthy cause; who at best knows achievement and who at the worst if he fails, at least fails while doing greatly, so that his place shall never be with those cold and timid souls who know neither victory nor defeat.

Theodore Roosevelt

The Individual Effects of Trauma

It is amazing the traumas that a person can survive. But the trauma alone is not the tragedy. What is tragic is what happens inside our minds when the trauma occurs and after it has passed.

From the outside looking in, it may seem easy to understand who the perpetrator is and where the blame lies. For those that survive, the vision is not as clear.

> Unfortunately, we ended up blaming ourselves and in a lot of cases, we blamed people that were safe to blame.

I didn't think that it was enough to ask about what happened, but to ask how it harmed each of us...how our thoughts and hopes about the future changed.

The tragedy is in our experience of the trauma. We harmed ourselves through depression, self mutilation, attempted suicide, drug abuse, and sought unhealthy sexual encounters.

The tragedy is that in most cases, we had nowhere to turn.

And, in having nowhere to turn, we blamed ourselves.

Why was this experience debilitating for you?
and
If you haven't already, please try to explain your thoughts and hopes about the future as you were experiencing your personal trauma.

Embarrassment, Humiliation, Silent Suffering (Depression), Daily Pain, Not Feeling Complete

Dr. Donna Thomas-Rodgers: At 19 years old I was just coming into my own. While my friends were in college discovering who they were becoming, I was faced with a daily challenge to conceal my hair loss. I was embarrassed and humiliated for years. I was mistaken for a man constantly. I did not date because men refused to understand my situation. I walked around bald for 2.5 years to show the world that I was beautiful without hair. I suffered silently and never really talked about my daily pain with my family until I began to write about the loss. No one knew how much it hurt to watch my hair fall out daily. There is so much pain in losing your hair. It defines you as a woman and when you lose it, you no longer feel complete. I felt like for years part of me was missing. I had to work from the inside out to begin to heal. It is still a work in progress but I want to share my story so that others can know that they are not alone.

I wanted my hair to grow back and I put a lot of time and energy into products and dermatologists. I hated going bald. Each day I wanted to believe that my hair was going to grow back. One day I was told that it would never grow back and I went home and shaved the remaining hair on my head off and I walked around bald for two years. Prior to that I had spent almost 10 years covering up my hair loss, I walked around bald to confront the shame and stares that I had endured over the years. All I ever wanted was hair all over my entire head and it never happened for me. I could not understand why. I just knew that I would have to come to accept the loss and learn to live with it. This is where I am today. Accepting and healing.

Lack of Awareness

Linda Norton: There is too much to try to say, in answer to that, to be able to say it with any kind of comprehensiveness. I spent the first 17ish years of my life pretty much in a coma. I spent the next 20 coming out of that coma; little by little... being reborn, in many ways. I've spent the past 13 years or so really living, and at last becoming the woman of power that God created in me.

Depression; Lack of Motivation; Loss of Hope

Pam Lontos: I couldn't get out of bed and had no motivation to do anything. I had no hopes for the future at that time, which is what kept me in a state of depression.

Insecure; Alone; Poor Choices; Fearful; Cynical

Ungenita Prevost: It made me very insecure. I really didn't know who I was or how I was supposed to be. I never felt connected and often times didn't know how to connect even if I wanted to. I sought out to get attention which often led to more complications in life. I befriended the wrong people and couldn't attract the right people if my life depended on it.

I was afraid, overtaken by fear during those times. I definitely had a glass half empty mentality and focused more on the negative aspects of my life. It wasn't a pretty picture. I would say "Why Me?" often.

Distrust; Low Self-Esteem; Shy; Frustrated; Angry; Physical Ailments; Fantasy World

Dana Detrick: It definitely left me with a sense of distrust and the kinds of self-esteem problems it would take a long time to overcome. I was blessed with many talents, and I was very shy about sharing them with the world because of this. The level of frustration I felt about not being able to change anything I was going through was something that it was very hard to shake, too. My anger management and patience are both things that I don't take for granted now. I also ended up with a few physical issues when it was all said and done, the worst involving my jaw. Over the years I've had instances where it locks up, and most of the time it pops and crackles quite a bit.

I went into a total fantasy world, but it was one that I always thought of as being my future. I had a beautiful life there where I was grown and away from it all, with abundance around me, and the calm and quiet I longed for. I would be the performer I wanted to be, I would be beautiful, and I would be loved and safe. These are things I always carried with me, and I don't know where they came from. I'm just very glad they were there. And as long as I kept them inside, she [my mother] couldn't destroy them.

Allergies; Asthma; Depression;

Dr. Barnsley Brown: Mentally and emotionally, I was neglected and taught to believe that I could not have a happy marriage that would last and a happy family with normal children. I have also suffered from allergies, asthma and mild depression for many years, probably since I was a child, and I control this now with exercise, acupuncture and other integrative healing methods, positive thinking, and a medication that actually works for me. I have combined the best of Western medicine and integrative medicine with my FAITH, and I am a survivor!

I did not realize the extent of my trauma until I was in my early twenties in graduate school and then a very frightening car accident introduced me to the Reiki method of natural healing that became the beginning of my road to healing, a road that continues to unfold today. It took another trauma, the accident, to bring up the deeply buried traumas of my childhood. I know now that all that I have experienced enables me to be the person I am—to coach others and help them heal the past and move forward with joy and courage. And my memories and stories reach out and awaken the memories and stories of my audiences when I speak, allowing them to bring forth their inner wisdom and power and to heal what needs to be healed.

I am at peace with what happened to me after much hard, hard work on myself and because of what I will call the unconditional love of the Universe which I experience through my beloved grandmother, Ruby! (And that's another story for us to get into...)

Repressed Memories; Dysfunctional Relationships; Low Self-Esteem; Embarrassed; Ashamed

Katie Custer (Chakra Girl): It was actually the experience of living with repressed memories that was the debilitating part. I have active, "normal" memories representing my life from age 12 until now (I'm 36). I have very little memory of life before that. Debilitation came through every day dystunctional relationships with family, friends, boyfriends, girlfriends, food, money…um, yeah. Through my teens and twenties, I did not allow myself to feel much confidence (I could put on a great show – nobody knew there were issues) because I didn't believe I deserved better. The confusing part (most debilitating, perhaps) was that I did not know why I felt that way – just that I was convinced that I shouldn't even try.

To elaborate, my self-esteem was very low. I felt stupid regularly and then stifled it because I didn't want to let on I was feeling that way – very embarrassed and ashamed of myself all the time. As a teenager, the hope I had for the future was the one positive glimmer on the horizon. Don't get me wrong, I was holding my own quite well – I was creative, funny, clever, etc. I also "knew" I wanted to move out of my house, get on my own and then, well, I had no plan. My home was a safe place to be a homebody, to hide. So the future did not have definition at all – I knew I loved to make art and be freely creative, but I didn't have big dreams of being an artist or anything.

Insecure; Low Self-Esteem; Eating Disorder; Depression; Suicidal

Diane Lang: This experience caused me great pain. It made me a very insecure person – when I was a teenager, every day I would ask everyone if they were mad at me or hated me because I was so insecure. In return, I had few friends, very little confidence and ended up with an eating disorder, depression and was suicidal. I wished for death till the end.

Repressed Memories; Dysfunctional Relationships; Low Self-Esteem; Suicidal; Drug Abuse; Lack of Identity

Deidre Hughey: I was already quite withdrawn from being separated from my family during third grade. However, after being molested by the 19 year old, I became increasingly withdrawn, confused and scared. (This person was eventually incarcerated for raping women at knife and gunpoint. It's believed that I was one of his earliest victims.)

The Individual Effects of Trauma

Toward the end of the summer, I found that I wasn't able to sleep anymore and told my mom what had happened at the store. Her response was, "So, what do you want me to do?"

I didn't know the answer to the question. But more importantly, I began to think that what had happened wasn't that serious. I began to doubt my decisions, grew to mistrust people in general and became increasingly withdrawn with severe mood swings.

Eventually, I became so depressed that I began systematically harming my body and became suicidal. At the age of 16, I was admitted into a psychiatric institution in Virginia called Springwood Institute. My admission, though voluntary, came at a complete loss of privacy as I was assigned a personal guard to always be within an arm's reach of preventing me from hurting myself.

As awkward as this was, it was strangely comforting to know that I couldn't hurt myself and no one else could hurt me either.

14 weeks later, I was released into the world that put me there. Life still sucked and I began to believe there was no need for hell, we lived it right here on earth.

When I was 18, my mother informed me that she had not wanted to have children. I looked at her and told her that my sister and I knew. We were never physically abused, but to say that there was a lack of love would have been an understatement.

I continued on a slow downward spiral through sexual promiscuity, drug abuse and personal debasement. I believed that life was hell and that I would never live a life with happiness or find someone that I could share my life with.

I repressed a lot of memories and in my twenties, many vivid memories came flooding back in a surreal sea of flashbacks. Many years and situations in my past are still a fog.

I had absolutely no dreams for a future. I simply existed. As a matter of fact, because I had no hope for happiness, I didn't value my life and took risks that quite honestly had every potential to kill me.

Lack of Security; Mistrust

Shirley Cheng: My own physical disabilities and blindness are debilitating in the sense that I have to be cared for 24/7 like a baby; other than that, I do not allow them to hinder me from going after my gold medals in life or living life to its very fullest. Diseases can touch only my body; they cannot touch my spirit. My blindness is debilitating because it does not allow me to see the beautiful world or capture it in my artwork. But I will never let it truly disable me.

Because of the loss of my eyesight (but never my vision), I stopped going to school and received home-tutoring instead. I successfully did my work using just tape recorders (I would listen to my assignment and record down my answers and essays on tapes, and then they were given to my teachers in school to grade). I also wrote and calculated long chemistry equations in my head without Braille (I can't use Braille because of my arthritis).

However, I could not accumulate enough credits to graduate (of the credits I earned, my average was 97 GPA), so I earned my GED diploma instead. I took the entire GED exam, including mathematical calculations and problem solving, graphs, and an essay, again in my head without Braille; still, my exceptional 3280 on the test earned me a special recognition award.

Since I can't express myself through my artwork, I turned to writing. I became an author at age twenty, completing three books the first year. I use a screen reader on the computer that tells me which keys I type and reads what is on the screen. In spite of the fact that I can type with only my two index fingers, I can produce about sixty-five words per minute.

The custody battles my mother and I had experienced were terrifying to say the least. Not only was my life in danger but also I could not be with the only source of love and security: my mother. Mother and I have always been extremely close, like a pair of binary stars ever revolving around each

The Individual Effects of Trauma

other, so it would have been an absolute nightmare if we were separated for so many years. Who knows if I could even be alive to see the day when we could reunite.

The experiences were debilitating because it made us trust doctors less. I felt that I had no sense of security or guarantee when I visited doctors. I didn't know who might be the next doctor to take me away from the loving arms of Mother.

I was extremely thankful when I turned eighteen. At last, I can finally say "no"; Mother can say "no" without losing me. Thus, I have become an advocate of parental rights in children's medical care to help today's loving parents protect and keep custody of the children of our future. When doctors ask yes or no, parents should have the right to say no!

My unpleasant circumstances with the aides in school were debilitating in a way that there was always a shadow when I went to school. It could have been completely filled with sunshine. Instead, I was in my aides' hands--I relied on them, entirely, to care for my physical needs, such as taking me to the restroom, where I hoped I would not get physically hurt. But my hope was fruitless as many would bump my feet into walls, and they would also bump me into students while pushing me down the halls.

However, this shadow never hindered my ability to absorb knowledge. When I was learning and listening to my teachers, it felt like it was just me, my teachers, and my class...the aide was somewhere else. I focused on my schoolwork, and I was a top honor student, being on the Principal's List in high school (ninety-five average and above).

During every battle I have with my challenges, I always hope for a bright tomorrow. I do not struggle with life. I see life as my best friend, so instead of resisting it, I keep my hopes high, for I know there will always be a tomorrow. Although I may not have a happily ever after ending in this life, my greatest hope lies in the life after this one on Earth, if I would be so privileged.

As for living my life right now--it is up to me to make the most of my situation and make the best of what I have got, so I do my utmost in living the best life possible, spiritually. I know that no one and nothing can destroy my spirit if I do not allow them, so I keep my spirit high amidst hardship.

Everything passes, and so will my trials and tribulations. Why waste my energy on things that will be gone tomorrow? Plus, I know that there is always someone out there who is in a much worse situation than I, so I am thankful for what I have, what I can do, and the people around me.

Shy; Awkward; Ashamed; Alone; Low Self-Esteem

Patricia Alcivar: These experiences were devastating to me because I felt as if I was an orphan growing up with no real parents. The people I was supposed to trust as a child betrayed me in such a horrible way. They did not protect me and never showed me real love and an innocent child was robbed of their childhood. Growing up, I was extremely shy and protective. I always felt awkward, ashamed and out of place. I did not have any friends growing up and my self esteem was shattered.

Inadequacy; Suicidal; Emotional Pain

Trish Lay: When I was three, my adopted mother was holding me as we stood in line at a store. A gentleman in front of us turned to me and said, "What a pretty little girl you are..." I then replied with, "No I'm not, I'm adopted." At age three, the heightened awareness of my self-worth was very apparent. My feelings of inadequacy molded into everything I did: Relationships, grades/school, work, finances, weight, and health. For many years I struggled.

Up until 25ish, my future seemed to be going nowhere. After several suicide attempts, I didn't believe life was worth living and I certainly didn't want to live if I was going to struggle with the emotional pain of "who am I." Finally, one night I put life and death on the table. If life was to be chosen, I had to commit to making myself better and create a future for myself and never use death as an option again. If I choose death, I had to end it and end it now. I faced my demons head on that night, physically and emotionally, and made the conscious decision to make my life worth living. At that time, even though it was very small, I saw light in my future. It was time to get to work, let go, stop playing the victim within my life and get out of my way.

Low Self-Esteem; Post Traumatic Shock; Sexual Promiscuity; Suicidal

Dr. Glenda Clare: I have always suffered from a low self esteem. Throughout my life, I always felt that I was just not good enough. There was nothing about me that was particularly exceptional. My family considered me second rate at everything. I was black – and dark skinned. I was always told that I needed to marry someone who was light skinned for the sake of the children. I remember being given bleaching cream as a child to improve my complexion. I was the "lost child" in my extended family. I never said much – I tended to blend in with the furniture.

No one except my Aunt Ida ever noticed. She died before I completed high school. Before being raped, I did everything that I knew to do to be considered "a good girl" and stay out of trouble. I graduated early from high school because my grades were good. By the age of 16, I had completed college credits. No one in my family noticed. I did not attend my graduation. I did not receive any congratulations or gifts. I worked at the hospital. I found joy and fulfillment in my work. I loved it!

Today, I believe that I had post traumatic stress disorder (PTSD) after my rape. I felt so dirty. I remember my college roommate talking to me about the many showers that I took each day. After rape - I did only three things: sleep, shower and party. I also began my quest for love. In my mind, love and sex were inseparable. I looked for love in all the wrong places – never finding any fulfillment.

Each and every semester, I enrolled in school. I found that I could not concentrate on my science courses. I couldn't focus on too much of anything. As a result, I failed many courses. It was like I was stuck in the revolving door of enrolling and dropping out of school….never completing anything. I saw everyone around me succeeding and accomplishing their goals. Me – I was doing nothing.

I don't remember all of the details but I decided that I wanted to die. I had a plan. There must have been a part of me that did not want to die because I remember being near 6th and P Streets in Washington, D.C. knocking on the doors of all of the houses of worship in the area. I was desperately searching for someone, anyone with whom I could talk. I knocked on the door of churches, mosques – any door that I could find. I found no one.

As I began to walk home a terrible rain storm erupted. I began to walk home in the rain fully intending to kill myself. It was then, that I met my angel. He saved my life.

Low-Self Esteem; Fantasy Life

Revvell Revati: I felt abandoned by my father because of his death and because of my mother's way of handling it. As a result, I never had good relationships with men OR women or myself. I had low self-esteem.

I had a lot of dreams as I'd stated. I would buy magazines that talked about surfing and I had pictures of my favorite movie stars doing what I thought I wanted to be doing (I lived in Connecticut at the time). I would be up most of the night listening to my favorite radio station and writing them letters asking them to play some of my favorite songs and felt special when they mentioned the nickname I made up for myself.

Sexual Promiscuity; Fear; Anger; Self-Doubt; Alcohol Abuse; Drug Abuse; Loss of Self-Respect

Jillian Montes: The rape was a shock as it was something I didn't expect, you could imagine. I had nightmares for 8 months after the incident. I didn't report it as initially I thought it was my fault. When I told people about it, some of them didn't believe me, so I started to question if it really happened or not. But as time went on, I realized I had been date raped and it was too late to report it, so I felt. The experience was also devastating due to the fact that I started to not trust my friends or feel safe. I didn't trust men, but it didn't stop me from starting to sleep around.

When the incident occurred, and having many people not believe it actually happened, I had a lot of fear and anger. Once I realized the truth and that it did really occur, I started to doubt myself around any man and started drinking more and smoking pot more. And 4 months later another incident happened where I was so drunk that I was taken advantage of. After that occurrence, I started to ask myself, "How could I allow this to happen again? What was wrong with me?" At that point I had lost all self-respect and didn't have a care in the world.

Sexual Promiscuity; Insecure; Lonely; Confusion

Dr. Nancy Irwin: It really wasn't debilitating at the time, it was actually "empowering" (I felt special and important) and "funny" if you will. I now see clearly that that was my only healthy defense mechanism. It took years of promiscuity and isolation and insecurity and love/hate relationships with men to see what a terrible blow to intimacy I'd suffered.

Interesting how it all came upon me one night. I was living in NYC and was at a Broadway play one night; *Burn This* starring John Malkovich. During the play, he instructs someone to read his letter and then "burn this" so no one else can read it. That went through me like a shot. I raced out of the theatre and vomited on the street. All of a sudden memories of the preacher's letters to me through the years I was in college came flooding back. Each one was (as I see it now) a sex fantasy of his....how he wanted to marry me if his wife died....how he had the sex drive of a 25-year-old man (he was probably 50 by then) with his 13-inch penis, and more. All the letters closed with a "P.S. Burn this. No one else could understand what we have."

Then I began a long journey of healing through therapy, self-help books, and my continuing education and training in the field of sexual abuse recovery and prevention.

I was very, very confused. Here was this preacher telling me on one hand that I should stay a virgin, yet encouraging me to explore sex with him and with the boys I was dating at the time. He wanted to know every detail. I felt like a Madonna and a Whore all at once. So I just finally figured that I was "damaged goods" and that is all men really want anyway.....so I gave into the basic instincts, and threw myself into my musical studies (I am a trained opera singer). I figured I would just be a big opera star and have affairs and never marry, because who could trust men anyway? That poor preacher's wife.....I declared I would NEVER be duped into marriage like her! Imagine knowing your husband was sexually insatiable and fondling girls in his church.

Insecure; Unloved; Depression; Loss of Hope; Suicidal

Dr. Karen Sherman: I never felt loved, cared about, or good enough. I was constantly put down. My mother was never able to be available to me.

As a result of this background that continued into my adulthood, I cut off relations with my parents. I learned that my father died and was relieved – I was finally going to have a relationship with my mother that I was never able to have because he dominated and she was afraid to stand up to him. But shortly after we started our relationship, it became apparent that there was no mother there – she was an emotional void. This set off a horrible depression – my lifelong dream was shattered. At one point, the pain was so unbearable, I wasn't sure I wanted to continue.

Lack of Identity; Low Self-Esteem; Loss of Hope; Alone

"Sarah": I had no nurturing or unconditional love growing up from either my mother or my grandmother. I needed that soil for the seed of my soul to germinate, but it kept getting brutally clipped before it could take root.

As a person, I suffered from a lack of identity and confidence, and that impacted my early adulthood as I struggled to find that sense of place and personhood. It also impacted my ability to socialize outside the household, and it literally disabled my ability to trust men, too.

At the time, particularly during high school, I didn't have any hope, nor did I even dream of a future. I was locked in the hell that was the present when that stuff was going on. I felt desperate and felt totally alone in the world. And empty. It felt like everyone in the world was against me and I was in the bottom of a deep well, with only slippery steep walls surrounding me with no way out. It was one of the darkest feelings I've ever experienced.

Depression; Drug Abuse; Sexual Promiscuity; Low Self-Esteem; Alone; Generalized Anxiety Disorder

Melody Brooke: I completely withdrew into myself and became a different person. I lost my joy of living and started to collapse until my teacher, Mrs. Conner, came into my life. Then I tried very hard to act as if I was fine but really still felt like I had no real value as a person. My mother had a nervous breakdown when I was 15, and then was diagnosed with breast cancer when I was 16. I was expected to become adult-like but I couldn't. I broke and started using drugs and acting out sexually. Never believing I was worth anything, underneath a façade of confidence I was desperately alone. I could not let anyone of any quality really care for me when I didn't believe I had any worth. I couldn't let myself achieve my dreams because I didn't really think I deserved them. And, I have suffered with Generalized Anxiety Disorder my entire life. I didn't realize that was what it was, and no practitioner had detected it. It wasn't until I read a description of it in a magazine that I realized my ongoing sense of doom and underlying sense that everything could fall apart at any moment was GAD.

As young girl I really don't think I thought of the future, and I never had a sense of any future at all, except that I wanted to just disappear. My only real hope was that someday a man would love me. I guess my attachment was to the idea of being rescued by a knight–in–shining–armor who could make me feel more worthy than I believed myself to be.

Anxiety Attacks; Loss of Hope

Cynthia MacGregor: Well, gee, would YOU like to live in a near-constant state of panic (the anxiety attacks), feel like a freak (for twitching and making noises), have people shun you and/or imitate you, and wonder what kind of future you had?

I didn't know WHAT the future held for me. My theatrical ambitions had been shattered and though I had always loved writing almost as much as acting, it now seemed like a poor second-best at most. I didn't know what an anxiety attack was or that anyone else in the world had them (none of my doctors had bothered to tell me) till I was 18, had taken an apartment in NYC, and found myself living next door to a magazine editor who, as she told me, understood what I was going through with the freak-outs because she too suffered from anxiety attacks.

As a young writer, whom could I respect more than an editor—and Pat not only had a name for what I was going through (not the Tourette's—it would be more than another decade before I was properly diagnosed on THAT score!) but told me she had the same problem! Of all the vacant apartments I had looked at (and yes, in 1961 there really WERE a lot of vacancies in NY!), I had chosen the one next door to an editor with anxiety attacks. Some would have called it good luck, but I saw in it the hand of God at work to help me. And it gave me some hope for my future.

Unloved; Suicidal; Alcoholic

Jennifer: Everywhere I looked people were depressed and unhappy. I had to figure out what happiness looked like on my own.

My thoughts were that I am better than this. I wasn't sure what I wanted to do with my life. I only knew I was going to do something that helped humanity. I had this strong feeling inside of me that I couldn't explain.

Abandonment Issues

Diana DeRosa: Unlike most childhood traumas, I was not as aware of my situation but I think it changed me as a person. All I remember was being in the hospital screaming and crying and begging my parents not to leave me, but they did (as hard as it was for them). Back then that's the way they approached things.

I think it destroyed my ability to ever want to care about someone, to love someone, because the people you love get taken away from you. Later in life as my hip started to fail (I would one day need a total hip replacement), I ended up in a lot of pain. I limped and it was embarrassing when people would ask me why I was limping as it wasn't always noticeable. It would happen when I got tired. I kept doing all the things that I did but it was more painful to walk any distance.

The Individual Effects of Trauma

My life was truly changed forever when I got a total hip replacement. The results of that are solid walking, dancing and so much more which has given my life a new breath of fresh air.

I believe that my story is different than most. I don't know that I realized the huge effect what happened in my life had on me. I believe it destroyed my potential to ever get married because that meant commitment. Being so young I was not aware of just how major all this would be in my life. But it probably gave me a huge independence to go after my dreams.

I have traveled the world as a journalist (writer and photographer). I dance, which is one of my great passions. I rode horses for many years and still am very involved in the horse world although these days I don't ride any more. I feel that I have been blessed with a great life even if I never did find my soul mate (or haven't so far).

Confusion; Depression; Lack of Identity

Rev. Brenda Bartella Peterson: The childhood traumas robbed me of having a childhood and delayed my discovery of who I am as an individual. The adult traumas have required massive amounts of energy---physical, psychic and creative energies which could have been spent elsewhere had I not been losing those closest to me in devastating ways.

Some would say I have accomplished a great deal in spite of the traumas. I would say that marriages three and four were the biggest symptoms of the unhealthy behaviors that manifested themselves in my life. I would also say that the best and the worst of my life trajectory have been manifested in relationships in general.

I told my siblings that there were three routes out of our family--- education, therapy or religion; choose one and ride it. In adulthood, I realized that it really required all three and more to overcome the damage of childhood.

Therapy as a child was not available so I chose education and religion. I went to church at times when no one else in my family did. My mother said later that I had blinders on about getting a college education, meaning that NOTHING was going to stop me from getting a degree.

I absorbed the care and feeding of teachers like a dry sponge (see my essay on Community on Facebook). Fortunately, in spite of going to 14 different elementary schools, I had a rich supply of school and Sunday School teachers who filled that role in my life. I am eternally grateful to them.

~~~

If the stories in this book are weighing you down and you want a boost of immediate inspiration, please skip to Chapter 7: An Unexpected Future. When you're ready, you can come back to continue your journey...things are about to get better!

We thought that there was something wrong with us.

Our traumas changed us.

We blamed ourselves.

We needed help.

Chapter 5: Finding Our Way

All of us found something or someone to help us to look outward and begin healing.

If I speak with the tongues of men and of angels, but have not love, I am become sounding brass, or a clanging cymbal. And if I have the gift of prophecy, and know all mysteries and all knowledge; and if I have all faith, so as to remove mountains, but have not love, I am nothing. And if I bestow all my goods to feed the poor, and if I give my body to be burned, but have not love, it profiteth me nothing.
Apostle Paul (1 Corinthians 13:1-3, American Standard Version)

Finding Our Way

Every woman in this book found a way to thrive beyond what their past "dictated" for them.

As an adult, I have a very distinct memory of talking with my friend Diane, whom I had known since 5th grade. She told me that she loves me for the person that I was and had become. She also told me that from what she knew of my past, she was amazed that I had turned out "so great." When I asked her to elaborate, she said that no one would have blamed me if I had turned into a bitter, curt woman bent on anger and living a tragically lonely life...with cats. (Okay, I added the cats, but you get the idea.)

When I asked her why she thought this, she answered that it was difficult for her to imagine that I could ever move past my history. If was hard for her to fathom that I could let go and begin to heal.

I believe that if you took any one of the stories mentioned in this book, you could come to a similar conclusion for each one of them.

So, why didn't we stay in a place of suffering?

What made the difference for us?

I had come to my own conclusions based on my life, but wanted verification as a whole and asked each of the women this question:

What or who is it that helped you to overcome and move in the direction of healing?

The answers are rewarding in that it brings to light the beauty that surrounds us if we just allow ourselves to see. Each person was touched by something or someone outside of themselves. It took an outside force to move each individual to think beyond their past...to look outwards and move toward a place of healing.

Finding Our Way

In some cases it was faith or religion, in others it was self-help books or the kindness of another human being. Sometimes the kindness was found in relatives, sometimes friends, teachers, counselors or therapists.

In almost every single case, it was the love and care poured out by another that gave each of us the hope that our future could be different.

In every case, I'm grateful that each of us found the strength and the ability to share our stories here.

Self-Help Books

Pam Lontos: I went to a seminar where Zig Ziglar was speaking. I bought his motivational tapes and listened to them every day. I started following the things he said to do like listing my goals, changing my thinking from negative to positive, saying affirmations and visualizing success and quickly noticed that I was overcoming the depression.

Self-Help Books and Kindness of Others

Rev. Brenda Bartella Peterson: It has been a journey not a quick fix. During the years of my second marriage that was so happy, fulfilling, nurturing, remedial, I thought all the damage of childhood was healed. When my husband died of lung cancer, I was astounded at all the scabs torn off of old wounds by the newly inflicted wound of his death. It is at that point that I very intentionally sought therapy and worked hard with a couple of excellent therapists for many years to heal damage that I had not previously even named.

Two traumas that reared their ugly heads in that period were the insecurity as a result of my parents' many marriages and really unknown effects of being sexually molested as a 5 year old. Therapy and voracious reading helped me address these issues.

Faith/Religion

Dr. Glenda Clare: I do not care what anyone else says or feels – I know that I met my angel on the day that I contemplated suicide. He knew things about me that I had shared with no one. He knew that I was intending to kill myself. He knew specifics about my plan. He visited with me for three days making sure that I was okay. Then he went away – never to be seen or heard from again.

Weeks later, my old roommate was raped. I was pretty docile in regard to my rape. I never really talked about it. My mother told me that these things happen and that I needed to just get over it. I internalized my feeling, becoming very depressed. After my friend was raped – I began to feel things.

Finding Our Way

I recall being in the park – alone – in the middle of the night. If anyone had been around – they would have thought that I was insane. I was engaged in a fight. I remember crying, punching, scratching and stomping my rapist. It was the first time that I expressed any anger or rage. I began to get out some of the feelings that I had inside.

In the weeks to come, I started to see a counselor who helped me to expunge my record at school so that I could start fresh at another institution. In all honesty, although not the best thing – what helped me most was being an advocate for women who were raped. I volunteered as a rape crisis counselor when I returned to college to complete my bachelor's degree. I met and counseled women immediately after they had been raped through the court process. Women called me whenever they wanted to talk. I listened more than I talked.

In the years that followed, I learned more about rape and PTSD. In 2007, I testified before the Centers for Disease Control (CDC) as part of a special group created to address issues related to the spread of HIV/AIDS among African American women.

Immediately after my testimony, I was approached by women with HIV/AIDS that were in the audience. I was told that my story was their story. Pelvic Inflammatory Disease (PID) is a sexually transmitted disease. You get it the same way that you get HIV/AIDS. I did not get HIV/AIDS because the disease was not in my environment at the time that I was reacting to my trauma. That was luck – nothing more. My reactions were typical of someone experiencing the trauma of rape and/or incest. Such factors need to be taken into consideration when developing prevention messages.

Kate Whetten, a Duke University Researcher, was surprised by findings in her recent study. She learned that more than 70% of the people in her study of persons with HIV/AIDS were survivors of rape/incest.

Ungenita Prevost: I knew I wanted more but I didn't know how to obtain it. When I had nowhere else to go I turned to the church. It was uplifting and reintroduced me to my Faith. With my new found faith, I immediately delved into self. I started to pursue my dreams. Getting into the core essence of me was invigorating. I would read and write every day. It was a cleansing process that I feel completely healed me.

Patricia Alcivar: I believe that fear and faith helped me move forward….Ever since I was a little girl, I was always attracted to physical sports such as running, gymnastics, and karate. They were things that made me feel good and took me away from my awful life. I would imagine myself winning a race and the crowd cheering for me. I loved it! It made me forget for that moment of the life I was living, so I continued to day dream about people admiring me and seeing ME as the hero. That has always been in the back of my mind and after my father left, my mom would always say that I was no good and would never amount to anything. This was her mantra and it took all my will to not believe it. That made me so fearful beyond words. When I decided to leave at the age of 15 years old, I knew I had to prove her wrong.

Kindness of Others

Dr. Donna Thomas-Rodgers: My mother was a great supporter during the loss. But because I was hiding my pain I really never talked about it to anyone. Even after I shaved my head I still never talked about what it felt like walking around bald for 2.5 years. Once I started wearing wigs I was able to talk about it more because I changed my hair every day. I still did not talk about the pain of losing it. About two years ago I started talking little by little and once I began to write the book about it I really began to share how painful it was and still is. My family and friends support me now that they understand how much pain I was feeling as my hair fell out. I only wish that I had the courage to talk about it sooner. I could have begun to heal and helped others but I was too afraid to talk about it.

Dana Detrick: The most important thing I had was the fortitude to put myself first. When I was 20, and my parents were divorcing, I took the opportunity to also divorce myself from my mother, her family, and her problems forever.

Finding Our Way

I had a wonderful fellow at my side who has been my rock on my good days and bad, and I'm blessed that he is now my husband and partner in all things. With his understanding and support, I always feel sane!

Also at that time, my father and I chose to get some counseling together, which helped to set a solid path in place for the growth of our relationship based on mutual respect and the kind of "normalcy" we never enjoyed before.

I've also been very lucky to have in my life wonderful mentors who have provided that example and "family" that I could only dream was real before. They've given me the tools to make my life exactly what I want it to be.

Dr. Nancy Irwin: A dear friend in college who actually read some of the "Burn This" and assessed the situation when I could not. I laughed at this stuff, and he encouraged me to cut off the "relationship" and start examining what it was doing to me. I still was in denial ...sort of swept it under the carpet ...for about 15 years or so.

Dr. Karen Sherman: A combination of a really good therapist and an unbelievably supportive friend who never left my side. My husband also was still there for me as I started to come out of it.

Katie Custer (Chakra Girl): In high school I had an English teacher and cross country coach who provided many years of mentorship and support. I do believe he was pivotal in helping me hang on. Once I made it through to 31 and that memory surfaced, I turned to one of my Reiki teachers and he provided a safe space, once a week, for a few months, so that I could navigate through the surfacing memories. Then I attended eight weeks of ongoing group crisis counseling with a handful of women. Very powerful. Soon after I did that, I began seeing a shaman for counseling and he was pivotal in showing me I was stronger than I felt (especially being in the midst of new information about my childhood). He taught me how to take what I was learning, intellectually, about energy, and apply it to my

74

everyday life. He taught me how to see proof that I am no longer in danger. That meant I was able to start accepting that I was no longer a victim of external forces. All of this in the last five years. Woo hoo!

Diane Lang: My brother was very helpful and then believe it or not [I was able to help] myself. At 16 or 17 – I heard the therapist say I will be dead if I don't change and eat, and well something clicked and I woke up and started the process of changing but I don't know why.

Revvell Revati: In 1986 I met my teacher, Rocannon MacGregor. He saved my life. I did 16 years of weekly and group sessions with him. I'm still with him 23 years later taking movement classes which go beyond the movement but take in the understanding of what we're doing and why.

Diana De Rosa: I think I just went through life not realizing how it all had affected me and was simply determined to go after my dreams. Saying that I was blessed with two terrific parents who were always there for me no matter what [would be an understatement].

My mom recently passed (September 28, 2008) and that has been extremely tough, but I was still so fortunate to have her in my life. She made me believe that I could do anything. My dad is supportive in other ways. He'll always be there for you when the chips are down.

My brother David gave me the encouragement I needed when in my 40s my hip was failing and I had to get a total hip replacement. I was devastated and scared but he supported me through that difficult time in my life. My brother Vincent moved in with me and helped me just by being there.

Melody Brooke: In third grade I had an amazing teacher, Mrs. Conner. She didn't pressure me to perform; she focused on what I was good at, and what I liked to do. I drew a lot. It was all I could do well. She praised me and encouraged me in art, even getting one of my paintings in an All City show, where I won first prize.

Slowly I began to come out of my shell and she encouraged my reading by helping me find books I liked. She also encouraged me to write and hugged me. She made me feel like I was an acceptable, likable person again. She made me promise not to ever smoke cigarettes (which I never did). I struggled to read but by the fourth grade I was reading, and by the sixth grade I was reading at a 12th grade level.

Sadly, we moved to a different school district after third grade and I never saw her again. But I can tell you that I would not have graduated from High School, much less achieved a Masters Degree graduating Summa Cum Laude if not for Mrs. Conner!

Of course, in my 30's I started therapy and it has been invaluable in helping me change the way I think about what has happened and how I feel about myself. Bodywork was especially helpful in that it got me out of my "intellectual" self into my feelings and helped me understand the layers that make up a personality.

Now, in my 50's and finally finding a loving man who is capable of really caring for me I find myself moving through the last bits of the distortions and long held unconscious beliefs about myself within the context of our relationship.

Jennifer: Many people showed up in my life and helped me overcome. My ex-boyfriend's mother, Rosalie, helped me in so many ways I don't think she even knows how much I credit her for my success. Adriana, a mother I never had, helped me to realize I am someone that can do big things with my life. She taught me to be confident in myself. My parents helped me overcome things by showing me what not to do in life.

Cynthia MacGregor: Well, it certainly wasn't the five different therapists who mistreated me for my so-called "psychosomatic problem" and never once diagnosed Tourette's. Nor did they tell me that my anxiety attacks had a name or that other people had them.

I would first credit an anonymous person—to this day I don't know who my benefactor was—who wrote to the Tourette Syndrome Association in my name and said words to the effect of, "I think I may have Tourette's. Please send me literature." Which they did.

I received this unexpected package in the mail, opened it up, read about What Is Tourette Syndrome, and said, "My God, that's me! That's what I have! That's what's wrong with me!" I called the TSA to thank them for sending the packet and asked them how they had known to send it. Checking their files, they dug out the letter that had prompted the mailing and informed me that I had requested the materials. I had not!

They sent me a photocopy of the letter, at my request. I hoped the typeface (this was in the days of typewriters, not computers) would give me a clue, and indeed the typeface matched that of a certain editor I was friendly with (by now I was writing and editing for a living), but Irene denied it had been her. And general inquiries among my friends as to whom I could thank for this startling revelation brought no admissions nor even clues as to who it had been.

The TSA recommended I visit a pair of doctors affiliated with Mt. Sinai Hospital in NY. The doctors, a married couple (I think their name was Shapiro—not sure), confirmed I had Tourette's and put me on Haldol. But I found the side effects intolerable and discontinued it.

Fast forward a few years.

My friend Randy, a fellow escapee from the inept psychiatrist whom I most blame for misdiagnosing me, told me she was finding help for her problems from a psycho-pharmacologist, a therapist who, instead of asking Randy to lie on a couch and talk about her childhood, treated her symptoms with prescription meds...a somewhat novel approach at the time.

At her recommendation, I consulted with, and then put myself under the care of, her doctor, who through trial and error got me on the right combination of drugs to combat my anxiety attacks and agoraphobia. In less than a year I was 90% better. At the same time, he urged me to try the Haldol again for the Tourette's. I told him the side effects had been intolerable, but he urged me to stick it out a week and see if the side effects didn't ameliorate. I did. They did. He was right. And the Haldol helped--not totally cured but helped—the Tourette's. Time helped, too.

Many people with Tourettes find relief in middle age, and I was one of them. Though I still have vestiges of it, nobody notices. The twitches and noises are so minimal that even my Significant Other is unaware of them. For all intents and purposes I am cured of the Tourette's. My current doctor (not a psycho-pharmacologist—I no longer need one—I am speaking of my internist, my PCP) keeps me on the Haldol because he says, "Why take chances?" But I no longer tic noticeably at all.

The anxiety attacks and agoraphobia are a thing of the past too—and so are the meds with which I controlled them. I no longer need them. I am quite freed of that problem.

Kindness of Others and Faith/Religion

Dr. Barnsley Brown: So many people and things: Reiki, acupuncture, Thought Field Therapy, my favorite school teachers and those who trained me in various healing modalities, GOD, one particular therapist I worked with for several years, Al-Anon, Unity principles and the Daily Word...and my beloved grandmother.

Shirley Cheng: First and foremost, it is Jehovah God who grants me the power and strength to move forward. I'm brave as I know He's always there, guiding me, supporting me, and loving me. I'm a sheep in His green pasture, and He's my Savior, my Shepherd, and I will never be in want as long as I know Him. And second, it is the most special person and treasure (besides my own life) He has given me: my dear mother, who is the cornerstone and light of my life, the foundation of my happiness, strength, and success, besides my Heavenly Father.

Linda Norton: About 20 therapists... and then God.

Jillian Montes: Shortly after the second incident, I met a young man who was not into drugs and was very kind to me. He ended up being my high-school sweetheart for two years and he helped change my life. But once I got into college, I started with the drugs again and didn't have great relationships (all based on co-dependency).

It wasn't until I was 23 years of age that my life completely shifted. I became a born-again Christian and I also started doing "life" seminars. With everything I was doing in my life, I completely stopped doing drugs and found the most wonderful man, who is now my husband of 6 years. I was delivered from co-dependency, fear and unforgiveness.

Faith/Religion, Self Help Books and Kindness of Others

Trish Lay: Therapy, self help books, adoption support groups, energy healers, physics, astrologists, and various spiritual and religious outlets; I immersed myself into everything I could get my hands on. I was like a sponge. Whatever resonated stayed, and what I didn't need was squeezed away. I needed to not feel alone, I needed my feelings validated. As the universe is abundant, particular people fulfilling my special needs would appear in my life to guide me through what was necessary. As soon as the lesson was learned, the teacher left. To look back, it truly was miraculous to see the individuals who were only there to show me a way through. They gave me the tools I continue to use today.

Deidre Hughey: The most poignant moment that I can recall is when I was in the psychiatric hospital. My therapist, Dr. Carole Hertz, had talked me into committing myself with the promise that she would do her best to come visit me every week. This was quite a promise. Her office was almost an hour's drive from the hospital and over an hour's drive from her home. In addition, she was not allowed to conduct therapy sessions at Springwood because it was a closed system.

True to her word, Dr. Hertz came and visited me every single week. For the first time, I felt cared about. I began to feel that my life was valuable to someone. To this day, I believe that Dr. Hertz saw herself in me and that thought gave me the strength to have hope that someday, I would be successful too.

During the tumultuous years after my release, I became a voracious reader of self-help books. Eventually, I would come to know God, find the support of wonderful friends and start letting go of my past.

The next most critical person in my journey toward healing was marrying my wonderful husband. His love, kindness and patience allowed me to overcome my sexual trauma and confusion as he would hold me close and allow me to cry during many nights in the first year of our marriage.

Self-Reliance

"Sarah": You know, I've been through counseling to process the stuff that happened during my growing up years, and have been told repeatedly that what has happened to me is a fairly rare occurrence in overcoming the trauma. Most people in such a hopeless situation either find someone else in their lives that can provide the nurturing that they need, or they end up self-destructing. I did neither. Something deep, deep down kept pushing. Pushing me to keep trying. To hope. Just when I got down in the dumps and start to feel like everything would self-destruct, up it would push, and I would say, "Okay, self. Time to take a deep breath and see what we can learn from this."

At probably the most critical points when I needed it, I sought counseling to help me sort out things, but I had to do all of the hard work myself and face those things I feared most. And I did. And I grew because of it! And I have been fortunate to have amazing friends who were there when I needed them. The old adage: "You can choose your friends but you can't choose your family" rang especially true for me.

A few years ago, I was leaving a job to take a new position, and the office threw me a going away party. I was handed a picture they had of me, and all the staff had written alongside the photo words they associated with me. I was surprised and delighted! But one word really stuck out: Brave. I asked about that, and was told: "You are the gutsiest gal I know." I was completely floored. But when I look back, I do see how I have not let my fears hold me captive, and have kept pushing myself. Maybe in a strange, roundabout way, it's still my grandmother in my head telling me "You won't amount to a piece of shit" that pushes me to prove her wrong, but I have also found myself along the way.

~~~

Most of the stories have a component of another person that cared. It goes to show the power that we have in each others' lives...how much we can do to mold another's future and make a difference.

If you're reading this and you haven't found your "hope" or "caring" person, my wish is that you can at the very least, relate to one of the women in this book and realize that help and hope are out there for you.

We have hope for you.

Whoever you are, keep in mind that some people need more compassion and understanding than others, and until you really know a person, you don't know where they've come from and what they've been through.

We all need to take the time to care about each other, to reach out to each other and show compassion.

"Ora na azu nwa"

Nigerian Igbo Proverb:
"It takes a village to raise a child."

Finding Our Way

Chapter 6: Acceptance of Our Past

For the most part, we wouldn't change our past...this may be the most difficult chapter for you to understand.

Acceptance of Our Past

If you want the rainbow, you gotta put up with the rain.
Dolly Parton

There is no one in the world I'd want to trade lives with.
Cynthia MacGregor

Face Your Fears, Live Your Dreams!
Unknown

It's never too late to be what you might have been.
George Eliot

I took the road less traveled by and that has made all the difference.
Robert Frost

Acceptance of Our Past

Acceptance of Our Past

In my 20's, I wished above all else that I could live my life over. I didn't want to repeat any of it! Instead, I wanted to live it again knowing what I knew at the age of twenty. I would make all of the right decisions and keep myself from getting in harm's way. But if a genie appeared before me to send me back to live my life again without my newfound knowledge, I would have run in the opposite direction, prayerfully in the direction of a very high cliff and thrown myself off.

I would rather have died than lived through my life again.

Over time, the pain began to subside and in my late 30's, I had healed enough that I became determined to learn more about my past (the pieces that I couldn't remember).

I decided to make the trek to Virginia and seek out my childhood friend Diane. Diane is a wonderful friend and in a lot of ways, very much like a sister to me. Over the years, even though we lost touch during several phases of our lives, our relationship always seemed intact every time we came back together.

Diane filled in the pieces that she knew of and was amazed at how little I remembered. During our time together, she became very sad and apologized for not knowing more and not having been able to be more help when we were younger.

I began to laugh and hugged her.

"Diane, I wouldn't change a thing! I love my life! I have two beautiful children, a husband that I adore and adores me and I have amazing, supportive friends. I'm a national speaker, a successful business owner, the producer and host of a radio show, and I'm in the process of becoming a published author. I'm one of the happiest, most well-adjusted people that I know! My past has made me who I am. I don't want to live it again, but I don't regret that it happened...not anymore."

Acceptance of Our Past

In coming full circle, my life had begun to make sense. By overcoming my past, I was in a place where I could begin to be an inspiration to others.

I wondered if the same sensations that I felt were felt by other women survivors.

I had been given the gift to be able to give hope to others just as others had given hope to me.

"If you had a magic wand and could alter any part of your past, would you do it?"

Dr. Donna Thomas-Rodgers: I would not change anything about my past. I am the woman I am today because of it. Every moment and each experience has given me a tool to achieve growth and success and that is what life is all about, living, learning and growing.

Ungenita Prevost: Definitely not, all of those experiences laid the foundation for arriving in this exact place in my life. If I were to alter or extract a day or hour I could very well be living someone else's life and not my own.

Pam Lontos: This is a difficult question to answer. While I would not want to relive that experience, it did give me the strength to become who I am today.

Dana Detrick: Certainly I wouldn't wish any abuse on my young self, and there are certain events within my life that I wish hadn't occurred, though they were not from my choices. In the grand scheme though, this is what made me who I am. So in that way, there's nothing. I'm in the "now" with it!

Dr. Barnsley Brown: No, absolutely not. God has orchestrated exactly what my soul needed to come into my power.

Katie Custer (Chakra Girl): Not anymore. As the cliché goes, I wouldn't be the person I am had I lived a different life.

Diane Lang: None – I am who I am because of it.

Dr. Glenda Clare: I don't know. On the one hand – I would not be me if I had not had the experiences of my life. However, on the other hand –

happiness is something that has evaded me most of my life. I would like to know what it feels like to be loved.

Shirley Cheng: I would not change my life. I understand that it is God's permissive will that everything has happened the way it had, so I will not want to change any part of God's plan or will for me. God has been lovingly guiding and supporting me, bestowing a great dosage of strength and power upon me, enabling me to take giants step forward. Without Him, I will be powerless. The challenges I have had are merely exercising machines for my spirit. They are debilitating on the surface and will never touch the treasures within me.

Patricia Alcivar: As hard as it may be, I probably would not change anything from my past because it has made me the person I am today. Everything in this life happens for a reason and perhaps all this happened to me so I can help and inspire other women. Sometimes I do wish I had a loving mother as I think any child would. I miss not knowing what it would feel like to have a mother figure say "I love you" and then hug you and make you feel protected.

Trish Lay: No. I am incredibly grateful for my past. If it were not for ALL the situations and challenges I encountered within my past, I would not have the knowledge and persistence to pass on what I have learned. I am exactly where I want and where I am supposed to be in this moment.

Revvell Revati: Absolutely not. I am who I am because of what has happened and what I've done about it. In the midst would I have changed things/experiences? Sure. Now? No! I AM the creator of my life; I've paid my dues and now it's time for me to LIVE!

Jillian Montes: Absolutely not. I have learned so much from the past and the mistakes I have made. It is because of my past that I am the woman I am today and I love who I am.

Dr. Nancy Irwin: Not a thing. I believe that I "signed on" for all these experiences to grow, to learn, and to heal others.

Dr. Karen Sherman: Absolutely not! All these experiences have made me who I am today. They have given me a far greater understanding of others and have allowed me to be a better therapist. They allowed me to write, *Mindfulness and The Art of Choice: Transform Your Life* which is a self-help book that lets the reader know that she doesn't have to be a prisoner to her past. Rather, I offer skills to allow her to make permanent changes to create a life of choice, a life of joy! I truly believe I was meant to walk this journey because I was strong enough to do so and it would enable me to help others.

"Sarah": No. I am the sum of all of my experiences, and I have become the person I am today because of what I have experienced in my life. I like and accept who I am today, which means that my experience is something I must embrace and accept as well.

And one specific thing that happened really changed my life, and I want to explain why this is a significant example: When I was getting beat up daily in high school for having a different accent, different clothes and different skin color (I am Caucasian but my skin is olive and when I tan, I am quite dark), I had a life-altering experience that has shaped me to this day. I was called the "n-word" by these small-minded and biased kids.

What happened there in the rough halls and sidewalks of my high school gave me an insight to why it is so wrong to discriminate against anyone. My mother and grandmother were bigots, and threw out the "n-word" a lot at African American players while they watched football. My grandmother told us stories in disgusted tones about how when she was younger, her skin tanned into a deep color, and oftentimes was mistaken for being black. She sneered describing how men would approach her, a white woman. How dare they! I was also forbidden to play with an African American playmate that I had when I lived in Louisiana.

Acceptance of Our Past

In fact, I remember to this day the tears in the eyes of Dionne's mom, Anna, when I had to tell her I couldn't play with Dionne anymore because she was black. I realized, as an adult, how wrong discrimination is from first-hand experience. My sister came to the same conclusion, and we both are committed to equality of everyone in a perspective that many people of our race don't have. And I would never want to change that because in a small way, now I know what people of color have had to deal with their entire lives, and how wrong it is.

Linda Norton: No. I would not be the sturdy and solid tree that I am today without enduring and learning to survive the hardships. As Stockard Channing said in the movie *Where the Heart Is*... "The Lord gives us obstacles."

Cynthia MacGregor: Good God, YES! At best, I'd remove the Tourette's and agoraphobia from my experience altogether; at least, I'd have everything diagnosed correctly immediately. I know if I'd merely KNOWN what was wrong with me it would have helped. I might not have FELT any better but I'd have COPED better. I'd have felt better ABOUT MYSELF.

Diana De Rosa: I wish I had met my soul mate and had kids but then again if I had my life would have been totally different and I am happy with who I have become, where I have been and where I am going.

Rev. Brenda Bartella Peterson: Yes, I would like to have my son back. Other than that miracle, I would request nothing. The events of my life have shaped me and I am happy with who I am.

Melody Brooke: Why would I want to do that? I would not be who I am today. Even my failed marriages provided me with the incredible gifts of three amazing women for daughters. My past has given me a unique perspective on relationships, on life and on experiences that no other human being possesses.

Jennifer: No, I believe everything happens just as it was supposed to whether it seems that way or not. I have learned so many things from my past and wouldn't change a thing. It has made me a better person.

Yes, this chapter may have been a surprise for you unless you've already turned the corner and reached a level of healing in which you're ready to give hope back to others.

If you're not, know that it's within your grasp and someday, this chapter will be yours to claim, too!

Acceptance of Our Past

Chapter 7: An Unexpected Future

Our lives are nothing like we were promised from our traumas.

We've moved from victims to heroes.

An Unexpected Future

Determination will get you further than talent.
Stephanie Damore

Nothing ever changes if nothing ever changes.
Unknown

A woman who is convinced that she deserves to accept only the best challenges herself to give the best. Then she is living phenomenally.
Maya Angelou

We fall down but we get up.
Unknown

If you don't try, you can't succeed; if you do try, you might surprise yourself.
Cynthia MacGregor

An Unexpected Future

An Unexpected Future

The lives that we live now are beyond our expectations. Some of us had been so profoundly affected and haunted by our pasts, that we are living lives beyond what others expected. In some cases, we not only surprised them, but ourselves as well.

Every person in this book has struggled, fallen and gotten back up. Sometimes we got up on our own; other times, we had someone give us a hand. In every case, we kept moving forward.

> We are no longer victims of our pasts
>
> and you don't have to be, either.

As I was pulling the stories together in this book, I realized that many of the women in this book have become my heroes. I am confident that as you read this chapter, the telling of where these women are now in their lives, that they would become your heroes as well.

If you're struggling right now in your life and your story resonates with one of the women depicted in this book, my hope is that this next section will give you the inspiration you need to go get help.

> You are not alone and there is hope
> for a wonderful future for you.
>
> Your search for a better life gives value
> to each of the women in this book.
>
> **Your healing gives our stories meaning.**

An Unexpected Future

What is it about your life right now that is different than you or others expected? (Please share your feelings and thoughts as well as the "what".)

And...

What is it that you are most grateful for in your life right now?

Dr. Donna Thomas-Rodgers: I am open and honest about the hair loss. I tear up some times when I talk about it, but I share my story whenever possible. I want people to know that they are not alone. Whether they have alopecia or cancer they are not alone. They are still beautiful and their hair does not define them. I encourage people all of the time. I live my life as an example of not waiting 15 years before you begin to share your story and healing. I tell them to talk about it. Buy a journal and write about it. The healing comes from being honest. I am better because I share the story. It really is a part of my healing.

I am grateful for life. At one point I did not want to live. I am glad that I am here to raise my daughter and share my life with family and friends. I am grateful for everyone that grows their hair and donates it to make wigs for people like me. I am grateful to share my story with anyone who has experienced hair loss and feels lost.

Ungenita Prevost: I never imagined myself to be a leader. Within the last couple of years constantly working on myself has allowed me to develop into a leader in both of my businesses. I have reinvented myself in a way that seems unbelievable. My new passions are writing and public speaking. I love the role of feminine inspiration. I have a beautiful home, friends, husband and dog. A completely beautiful life from the inside out...it's pure bliss.

I am blessed to have internal health and the healthy relationships that I have developed with friends and my Mother.

Pam Lontos: From my upbringing, I felt like I was worthless and never expected to become a person that other people would come to for advice. I now have two books and still do some public speaking. It's amazing that I still have the same brain and education as I did when I was depressed, and now here I am with a successful public relations firm and two books. The main thing that changed was my attitude.

I am most grateful for knowing that I am in control of my life and I'm able to spend time with my husband and family.

An Unexpected Future

Dana Detrick: Certainly I don't think my mother or her family thought I would ever cut them out of my life. I had been conditioned for so long that their immorality was normal and acceptable, as clearly they were passing it on from generation to generation. I think they expected me to eventually "get over it", y'know? But I wouldn't trade the life I have now for anything, especially not the risk of having to go through any of it again! It's been almost 15 years now, and I can't see a future that would involve any of them.

I have such a fun, wonderful life now, and I could say so many things, but really, I think "peace" is my number one goal. The volume of my life was so loud as a child, and having calm and silence is such a simple joy. I have a great husband, amazing animals that inspire and entertain me, and a growing business that is my passion. I can't imagine anything greater!

Dr. Barnsley Brown: I'm married with a biological child, whom I had at the age of 40, all naturally—what a beautiful birth we had! And I am no longer the one everyone pushes around or walks on—I am a WOMAN of POWER and I teach others how to become women of power and to live the mission that God gave them.

And by golly, I am the first woman PhD in my family, another enormous achievement that no one expected. And I speak to thousands of people in my work. Many things are different than what folks expected or tried to convince me was true.

I am most grateful for my daughter, Zilia, and my new loving family -- my husband, his mother, his sisters and brothers, and all the other family we have in the U.S. and Peru.

Katie Custer (Chakra Girl): I never expected to find any kind of work that I love doing – massage therapy. Actually, I found that work before I ever learned about energy...and found it within months of hitting rock bottom. Learning about energy was life changing b/c it showed me why I was so stuck, depressed, obese, and why my debt load kept growing despite my "best efforts".

Once I started remembering things, I also started journaling regularly. Journaling turned into writing books. Underneath all of the junk, it turns out I'm not only an artist, but also a massage therapist, energy healer, and writer (which also makes me a teacher). These last few months I finally landed in contentment. I know that I can keep up this inspired life; I know that I deserve it all, and I know that I created all of it myself.

The best part, at that point, was seeing proof that I was on the right track because I started attracting people who were ready to do their own healing work. I could be a guide for them (teacher) and also recognize that they had something to teach me (student).

This past month, an additional sprinkle of magic has been added – I met someone who is one of the most beautiful people I have ever encountered. Having him in my life, I recognize that he is yet another mirror of the Self I am now radiating into the world. I never thought my life would look like this – never dreamed it was possible. And I know that I'm only at the leading edge of it, too.

It is simultaneously exhilarating and freaking me out. Because of the latter, I just returned to serious, daily meditation. I know that the more fantastic my life gets, the more old stuff will be felt as it is left behind. That emotional stuff is f***ing hard. (Too candid? Ha ha!)

My life, period. I'm grateful that I chose to stay alive in the moments when I gave myself an option. So...maybe that means I'm grateful for my Self? In the long list of blessings running through my head (every person, event, even every time I got hurt), I guess that right now I am most grateful that I made the choice to stick it out. Hope was so tiny in me in my darkest moments, like a grain of sand. Hope is powerful.

Diane Lang: I have a graduate degree and I teach college and I published a book – no one thought I would accomplish anything because I was so down, depressed and insecure. I didn't even think I would end up being anything at the time.

An Unexpected Future

My daughter and my new view on life and how that view has helped me empower other women.

Shirley Cheng: Although nearly nine years have passed (has it really been that long?), it still surprises me that I am blind. Even though I am by no means depressed (I have never been, even when I lost my eyesight), it is not a thrill, either, though it itself has brought me much thrills.

For one, it has turned me into an author. Surprisingly, I feel that I am the most surprised of all of this fact. When I was in middle school, it felt like every one of my peers urged me to become an author when I grew up. But my mind was made up on becoming a visual artist and famous scientist to find cures to all the devastating diseases out there. So now I guess the joke is on me! I have become what everyone thought I should be because they loved my writings.

Frankly, I would not have chosen to be an author if I had not lost my eyesight. But since I could not express myself in my artwork and I still want to pursue the arts, I turned to writing to share with others my imagined worlds and creations. I know this is in God's plan for me, and I cannot say it is a bad plan at all, either. Although I would rather be sighted than blind, I am able to touch others with messages of hope and inspiration through my writing.

This divine turn of events has given me this special opportunity, I believe. Otherwise, I would have just gone to college and graduate, not touching people's lives the way I am now. Is it my calling? I do not know, but one thing I am certain is that I will just leave it to God to take my hand and lead the way, as I enjoy every second of my exciting journey.

I'm extremely grateful to be alive; I'm so honored that God has chosen me to live so I can experience all the wonderful things life has to offer. Compared to the entire universe and all the beauties it contains, my problems are tiny! I'm never scornful for losing my eyesight and the ability to walk; instead, I'm simply grateful for having owned these powers before.

104

Plus, I'm still the owner of so many other great gifts: I can still hear, I can still talk, and I'm still alive, so I utilize all these treasures to become an award-winning author and motivational speaker to touch as many people as I possibly can to bring humor, hope, and healing. I'm also extremely grateful to God for giving me the best mother anyone could ever ask for. She is the world to me!

Patricia Alcivar: I am so grateful to say that I have now overcome the odds. So many girls that have been sexually/physically/mentally abused have turned to sex, drugs, and alcohol to forget and not face their past and fears. I am one of four sisters and even though my sisters did not get sexually or physically abused, they witnessed my father being an alcoholic and being a monster to both me and my mother.

My three other sisters are struggling single moms and two of them did not finish high school. I am the only one out of them who went on to finish two years of college, had a beautiful dream wedding, and I am living a healthy life and marriage with a bright future ahead of me. This is definitely not what my mother, family, or neighborhood expected of me or any girl growing up in that poor environment.

I am grateful to have a wonderful husband who is so different than any of the men in my family. He was born in Queens, NY but his father is formerly from Israel and his mom's ancestry is Irish/Italian. Growing up, I promised myself never to get involved with a Hispanic man with such old school mentality. My husband, Brian is supportive of my goals and dreams. We love to run and set goals together and he does not hold my past against me.

My dog, Jack, has also been a blessing to me. On my hardest days all I have to do is look at him and smile...I see Jack as truly something precious without a mean bone in his body. Growing up with my family in that horrible environment and then living in rough New York City, I did not think anything precious existed until I discovered animals and Teddy Bears.

I am grateful for the life I have now where my husband made the wise choice of relocating to Asheville from New York City. It has been challenging for me to adjust, but I have the wonderful opportunity to go back to school, enjoy the wonderful mountains, and finally have a beautiful home.

Trish Lay: I NEVER thought I would be a happy person. Living in such a dark place and having constant negative thought patterns, I often felt doomed and ruined. The fearful thoughts, anxiety, and stress I once had has been replaced with thoughts of love, forgiveness, joy, and faith. Granted, I am human...I still have emotional and situational curve balls thrown at me; regardless, I now have ways to deflect and not allow my past to influence my future. My inner strength and self propelling confidence is overwhelming.

God. My life. Having the courage to face my fears and know within, I matter to me. It is not significant how others see me; I know who I am now. Having the sound understanding and awareness that no matter what happens in my life, I can face it with self-belief and strength of mind to know everything is going to work out exactly the way it is suppose to.

Faith. After attempts to end my life, it became very obvious to me I was supposed to be here. And I am grateful for the opportunity to live and build the best life possible.

Dr. Glenda Clare: I did not become Glenda Clare, MD. Through God's grace, I did become Glenda Clare, Ph.D. I am not a psychiatrist; however, I am clinically trained to provide therapeutic services. I am no longer someone that has nothing to say, hiding in the shadows – the "lost child." I have a great deal to say about a number of things that make individuals and families fragile. I have much to say about the impact of trauma in a person's life.

I am most grateful for the presence of God in my life. I know that he has always loved and protected me – when no one else cared.

Revvell Revati: Everything is different! I just turned 60 living 20 years longer than I expected. I have my own business which includes international speaking, mostly to women about raw food/healthy living; I have five podcasts/online radio shows plus a membership site; I can breathe freely; I've been married for over five years (first marriage) and every day is worth living!

Life. I write appreciations DAILY. I've got a thread on one site that has about 66,000 views. I've gotten others to write appreciations. Learning to look around and FIND things to appreciate every day is a blessing to me.

Jillian Montes: The biggest thing that is different in my life is the fact that I have learned forgiveness. I was not one to let go of things, nor forget about them. I would hold things over people's heads to get what I wanted and was manipulative. Now, I don't do that any longer, nor do I struggle with forgiveness, hurt or pain.

I am most grateful for God, my husband and even my past. If it weren't for my past, I would not be where I am today which is happy, healthy and overjoyed to be alive.

Dr. Nancy Irwin: If someone had told me 25 years ago that I would be a psychologist, I'd have laughed in their face! Most people, myself included, assumed I would be on TV and stage as an entertainer (comic, singer, or actress). Obviously something was missing for me in entertainment....just wasn't the best fit. Thank God my community volunteer work woke up the healer in me. That has helped me heal more than my own therapy, I believe. Fortunately, my stage and screen experience serves me in my public speaking and media appearances, and allows me to inject humor, when appropriate, in the clinic.

Most people are excited about my being a therapist and working to help the sexually abused, yet I feel many believe I have exaggerated my own abuse. While it certainly is an uncomfortable subject to discuss outside of a therapy or medical office, sometimes we victims need acknowledgement of our own feelings and responses to our own pain.

An Unexpected Future

My health and fitness; my book; my friends; my family; my thriving private practice which affords me the honor of inspiring others on their path to healing.

Dr. Karen Sherman: I am more positive, I don't react emotionally any more, I can enjoy life as I never did before, e.g. appreciating nature and having fun.

I'm grateful for having the life I do – my inner strength, my family and husband, my life.

"Sarah": Once in a while, I sit back in my office and think to myself, Oh my God. How in the world did I become so successful after such a crummy life I started out with? I look at all of the work I've done, and the accolades I've received, and examined how much meaning I've found in the work I've done and the satisfaction I've gained from doing my very best and helping people, and I realize that I turned out more than okay. I've turned out great. I'm successful. I've got a great business reputation.

My second husband is the true love of my life – I am deliriously happy with our life together. My first marriage ended up so amicably that it is the envy of many other divorced couples, and we end up getting together as couples every so often without a stitch of "weirdness" – it's great!

My life is full of wonderful, caring friends who would drop everything at a moment's notice (and I would do the same for them). These people I treasure. My sister and I get along wonderfully. Sometimes I have a moment where I wish I could go back into time and tell that scared little girl that was me who had not a hope in the world that everything is going to be okay. I feel like I am able to have "retroactive compassion" for myself for all the times I had so much despair.

I am grateful for myself and the person I have turned out to be. I have worked hard to rid myself of the anger and sadness from the trauma I suffered as a child, and have worked through much of my issues. My grandmother suffered a stroke, which took the mean edge off of her, so we made our peace.

I went through counseling, and realized that my mother has borderline personality disorder, and I don't have to accept her anger and frustration into my life nor her manipulation. My first marriage ended incredibly amicably; I avoided the pitfalls of man-hate that my mom encouraged me to feed on. My drive to succeed has allowed me to arrive in a place where I find meaning in my work while providing value to those I serve.

My second marriage is full of laughter and joy, and the little stuff that used to drive me up the wall in my first marriage simply doesn't matter anymore. I can have good times and bad times, and still feel positive about everything in my life as a whole. My friends are my family and we are there for each other when we need it. I am grateful to have found love. To have found myself. And to like myself.

Melody Brooke: As a child, the one thing I craved and felt would never come my way was a "someone" who would love and care for me. My first two husbands said they loved me but were unable to express it in any way that felt like love to me. I divorced my twins' father in 1993 and did not remarry until 1999. I had given up hope but there he was, a 5'7" sweetheart. Together we have almost finished raising our (together) five children. My oldest is a lawyer in San Diego and happily married. One twin is in Taiwan studying Chinese and teaching English, the other is in Edinburgh, TX working in a library studying to be a librarian. Mike's oldest is in her junior year at NYU and his son is finishing 8th grade here in Lewisville. Our bond grows stronger every day as the different parts of me accept that he really does love me.

I am most grateful for the love that has helped me survive. God's love lived buried inside me for all these years, and it carried me through. The love in my life from God, inside of me, my husband, my children, and my friends transformed how I view myself and my world.

An Unexpected Future

Jennifer: Everything! No one expected anything from me. I own two companies now, have lived in Hawaii and made six figures by the age of 21. No one expected that.

I am most grateful for myself and the wisdom I have acquired. Oh, and Yoga has helped me become more grateful for my physical self.

Linda Norton: This is another "gosh... where do I start" answer. I'm probably the one who would have been considered "least likely to survive," "least likely to stay out of jail," "least likely to do much of anything." Instead, I've done a whole lot, and I've helped a whole lot. There are so many things that I still want to do... traveling among them, learning to fly a plane, become completely fluent in Spanish (I'm about 25% there.)

But I have raised awesome children, succeeded way beyond most people's dreams (even without an education), and been elevated (by God) into a position of authority where I can help other people find themselves, find and embrace the beauty that God instilled in them, and ultimately to succeed.

The relationship that God has allowed me to have with Him; it's the most intimate and beautiful part of life imaginable. The children that He has given me, and the angels that surrounded them (quite literally) as they were growing up. The angels that continue to guard my family, and the love and faithfulness of the Holy Spirit in every minute of every single day.

Cynthia MacGregor: Well, actually when I was a kid, half the people who knew me (and my ability for writing) expected me to grow up to be a writer. But I didn't expect it. I had my heart set on acting. And when that avenue became closed to me, I didn't think I had much of a future I cared about at all. I was resigned to merely plodding through life. My career choice had been closed to me. I was a freak who twitched and made weird noises. I was beset by terrible anxieties. I was often afraid to leave the house. What kind of future could I have?

Nonetheless, I was determined to move to NY and live on my own, though resigned to a nothing of a job instead of the exciting acting career I had envisioned. But I moved to NY, took an apartment, took an office job, continued to write (I need to write like most people need food) and, through being in the right place at the right time, found a paying outlet for my writing through which I was able to make what was then significant money for me and then, again through being in the right place at the right time, landed my first editing position.

My life now: I am the happiest person you'll ever meet. Relieved of the Tourette's and the anxiety attacks and agoraphobia (I have other health issues now, but unrelated) I live a fairly normal life. I earn a living—I'm NOT rich but I can support myself—writing and editing, working from home (which was important for me in the agoraphobic/Tourette days, is still very helpful now that I have chronic diarrhea, and certainly is a very comfortable way to work for ANYONE, having no commute and all the comforts of home in one's workplace).

At 65 I have NO intention of EVER retiring, am always seeking new challenges, LOVE my work, LOVE my life...and try not to look back at the bad old days.

I'm grateful for:
1. A means to earn a living doing something I LOVE.
2. Being free of my Tourette's and agoraphobia/anxiety attacks.
3. The love of my Significant Other.
4. My friends.
5. My optimistic outlook on life.

Diana De Rosa: I believe that by now I would have expected to be married and have children. Instead I've lost that opportunity but have done a ton of things in my life. So, it's okay.

Having been blessed with two wonderful parents. Not everyone is that lucky. We were not wealthy in terms of money but we were surrounded by wealth in many ways. I'm also thrilled that I've been recognized by all I have achieved in my life and that others seem to appreciate my accomplishments and feel they are worthy of being recognized. I am also grateful I had the opportunities I did to travel the world, to work for Christopher Reeve, to cover so many Olympic Games, to do TV reporting, to partner dance and more.

Rev. Brenda Bartella Peterson: Many persons from different stages of my life would have expected a more public, more national, more famous career from me. Trauma, grief, two extraordinary sons have required much of the focus of my adult life. I do not begrudge these sons or the incidents of my life this focus. These events have created the person I am today and I'm content living in this skin. If I look back on the skills and talents that I possessed along the way, I may ponder what might have been but I do not mourn what might have been.

The effect of rearing two extraordinary sons (mostly by myself) has not been addressed in these questions because on most days I do not consider the effect of rearing them a "trauma." But it did present several traumatic events during those years that I chose to devote my energies toward them instead of a more focused devotion to career.

My life, my theology, and my practice of life have always been rooted in relationships. So I am most grateful for the relationships that enriched my life. There are many but I would single out two, my husband, John and my grandson, Tristan.

Deidre Hughey: I didn't expect that I would ever have the life that I have now. I believed that I would never get married and would absolutely never have children. And when I met Shawn, I didn't expect to get swept off my feet! Quite honestly, without the help of God and my friends, I may not have let it happen.

For the past 14 years, I've been extremely happily married to a wonderful, caring and loving man. I have two beautiful boys. I own my own business, write a column for a magazine, produce and host a radio show and have become a national speaker.

But by far, the biggest surprise of all is that I'm deeply happy and full of hope! I see greatness in my future and in the future of others. I have goals and dreams beyond my understanding of how to make them come true, and yet, I believe that they will happen!

My husband, my children, and my friends. I love them all dearly and their worth to me is immeasurable. I am grateful for who I have become and the life that I live and will continue to live. I am deeply grateful for all of the people that believed in me when I had given up. I am grateful for the knowledge that I am worthy of a wonderful life and worthy of the love that I now receive. I am grateful that I get to carry this message forward and prayerfully bring hope to those that need it most.

~~~

Most of us are living lives that we never imagined we would. We're happier than we thought possible and at times, thought we deserved. None of us in our youth could imagine that we would be living the life that we live now.

We hope that our success inspires you to dream...
to realize that more is possible than
you may believe so right now.

Join us.

An Unexpected Future

Chapter 8: Our Message to You

If we could meet you,
if you are struggling like we struggled...

this is what we would say to you.

Feel the fear and do it anyway.
Susan Jeffers

An investment in knowledge always pays the best interest.
Benjamin Franklin

Don't make someone a priority that makes you an option.
Unknown

Change is inevitable. Either accept it or affect it.
Dr. Nancy Irwin

Nobody is stronger, nobody is weaker, than someone who came back. There is nothing you can do to such a person because whatever you could do is less than what has already been done to him [or her]. We have already paid the price.
Elie Wiesel (1928) Activist and American (Romanian-born) author.

Our Message to You

I asked each woman if they had a magic wand and could alter any part of their past, would they do it? Why or why not? Almost every single woman said they would not change their past. Some of you may find that surprising. Why wouldn't a person want to change the past that caused them so much grief?

I think the answer to the "why" becomes more evident when you read the answers. Every woman feels that they have become better people as a result of overcoming their past. Each woman feels powerful and empowered.

Many of us have found ourselves in a place where we get great satisfaction in being able to help other women to find the strength to overcome as well.

To find hope again.

However, having overcome my own personal traumas, I also believe that most of us would not choose to live our lives again. (This is not a question I asked, but feel very strongly that given the choice, we would not live the traumas again.)

In knowing this, I believe that we don't want to see other women have to undergo the trials that we underwent. We don't want other women to feel the despair and loss of hope that can come with trauma.

I thought it would be interesting to hear what each women would say if they were to meet a younger version of themselves.

If you had the chance to talk to a woman in the throes of what you experienced, what advice would you give her?

Dr. Donna Thomas-Rodgers: I would tell her that she is beautiful. Inside and out she is a gem, a precious stone. I would tell her that her loss will make her stronger. She will be equipped to handle any situation. I would tell her to share her story, get a sponsor to talk to in the difficult moments. Find a support group and stay in it long after she is healed so that she can be an inspiration to others. Hair loss is not something that you should have to suffer through silently. There are thousands of people that share in this and can help you through it.

Ungenita Prevost: No matter how difficult your situation may seem there's an opportunity within your reach to turn your life around on a dime. I encourage you to not settle for less. Surround yourself with people who inspire you. Get a mentor. Read self-help books. The more <u>you</u> improve the more <u>things</u> around you improve.

Pam Lontos: Zig Ziglar says that you are what you are because of what goes into your mind and you can change who you are by changing what goes into your mind. I would tell her to read motivational books and listen to motivational CDs and do the steps that are in them such as setting positive goals and getting rid of negative thoughts.

Dana Detrick: Since I associate most of what I went through with my childhood and teen years, I would first tell any young girl to reach out to another adult if she can. It's just not always possible. People don't want to get involved, even when they do suspect.

Aside from that, we must all know that the events and circumstances of our lives and our births do not define us. The choices of others do not define us. We are made of spirit, and we can and do rise like a phoenix from the flames if we allow our inner voice to tell us that we can. Life can be what we want it to be. We can be Victors, not Victims.

Dr. Barnsley Brown: Get help! Get an incredible counselor to help you talk through things, go to Al-Anon or ACOA (Adult Children of Alcoholics), go to reputable healers who have great results and are recommended to you, learn REIKI and practice it every day (I've done this since 1992, for 17 years now!) Know that just because you didn't have a loving family doesn't mean you can't have one. You are invaluable on the planet and no one has the exact soul fingerprints that you have—it is your RESPONSIBILITY to become all you can be, and to do that, you must get help from others!

Katie Custer (Chakra Girl): Be patient with yourself. And inject love for yourself into the practice of patience. Be patient. At all times. No matter what. No matter who is doing what to you, no matter how daunting the challenge, be patient with yourself. Whatever you survived or are surviving, your energy body is taking on the load. Once you start making changes, your energy body will start letting go.

Sometimes it means you will be really emotional. It will leak, drain, whoosh, and sometimes explode (for me it's meant whimpering, crying, sobbing, and/or screaming – often into my pillow or in my car) out of you when you are ready to let it go. Other times, you will feel more joy than you EVER felt before – more than you ever thought you were capable of…more than you dreamed possible!

You might have gotten used to the patterns or behaviors you engage in w/others (family, friends, coworkers, etc) and they feel "comforting". They are predictable and that is what keeps you going. You do not have to make any changes right now, but maybe just start by asking yourself what you would want to do first "if" given the chance to make a change. Take one step, see how it feels. Baby steps still get you where you want to go.

Be patient. This is really hard. You are not only changing your life by letting yourself think differently, you are literally changing your brain chemistry. Retraining, re-parenting, and giving yourself permission to emerge as who YOU are. Once you give yourself permission to think differently (to dream, perhaps), you have started the process. Your brain is the most powerful tool you have. Nobody can take it away from you. Start there.

Our Message To You

Diane Lang: Don't give up – if I could do it – anyone could. I'm always honest as a professor and therapist and tell people I was abused and in my own hell. That is why I'm a therapist and I let them know how happy I am now.

Shirley Cheng: Count on God, for He knows what is best for you. Count on Him for giving you the strength, the ability, and the power to take one sure step at a time. When you have your faith in God strong and steady, your steps in life will be strong and steady in turn.

Patricia Alcivar: First, you have to have faith! Faith literally moves mountains and without faith, how can you have dreams? Second, believe in yourself no matter what! Find an activity that makes you feel good...whether it be dancing, hiking, running, swimming, etc. Take the time to treat yourself right because you are worth it. Take a course in cooking, learning a new language, or anything that will open your mind and heart to other new and exciting things. You can meet great people that can also help you get away from the everyday stressful situations.

Trish Lay: Be kind to yourself and give yourself room to grow, which means you must have patience. Find forgiveness for you and for those who may have hurt you in the past. You are in the current moment and those people can no longer hurt you, therefore, let it go – truly let it go. Find forgiveness and your heart will open to love yourself.

Dr. Glenda Clare: Stop and breathe! You have a right to feel whatever you are feeling right now – in this very moment. God loves you and that is all that matters. Pick yourself up, dust yourself off and move forward.

Dr. Karen Sherman: Do not be afraid to embrace your pain – it has been stored in your body as you experienced it as a child so when you consider it now, you think it will feel as bad as it did when you were a child. But when you face it, the pain will transform and it will help the healing.

Revvell Revati: Talk about it to SOMEone who can help yet feel free to change your story. Know that sometimes, some of the things we think are only OUR perceptions of them and may not be accurate. When telling your story, always ask yourself "Is this true?" "Is it REALLY true?" I carried stories about my mother and my perception of events that were just not true. They were part of MY story...not hers.

Get help. Know that sticking around is SO worth it! Life is valuable!

Jillian Montes: I would advise her to recognize that it wasn't her fault and to forgive the person who hurt her. That was the hardest thing for me to do was to forgive the man who raped me and even start to pray for him and hope that he has overcome the hurt and pain he has dealt with in his life. There is a saying that one of my mentors says, and it is "Hurting people hurt people." It is a simple, yet profound statement. Once you realize that the person who hurt you must have been hurting to do what they did to you, it is easy to forgive. I truly believe that we are all good until a situation happens to us that has us CHOOSE a certain path.

Linda Norton: Do not be afraid. Decide right now what you want, and decide that you will remain strong enough to do it. Survive for now if you must; but know that you will come out of this...and will be so much stronger for it. If you need something to do while you're surviving, get busy planning (in your own mind) how you're going to succeed. Then, when you're able...take the time you need to heal, then without pushing yourself based in fear...take one step every day toward your goal. Each time you can add another step, do it. And remember that God is real, and nearer than you can possibly imagine. Keep Him the center of your being, your work and your trust...and you will be free.

Cynthia MacGregor: Don't give up. There IS an answer out there. Keep looking till you find it. And keep believing that you WILL find it. Don't ever give up hope.

Our Message To You

Dr. Nancy Irwin: I do this for a living. Outside of the legal obligations (medical check-ups, reporting, arrest, etc.), I encourage the victim to embark on a path of healing, which generally includes:

Allowing her to tell her story, vent all her feelings (shame, guilt, etc.) and express her anger toward the perpetrator as well as any enablers. We begin constructing/designing her life through setting goals, establishing a healthy support system, nurturing and self-care (this is different from person to person depending on their health, age, spiritual beliefs, etc), setting up techniques to get through any triggers. We celebrate "wins" - - - in court, and in personal life (getting into a great school, a great relationship, etc.).

With immediate intervention, psychological damage can be minimized greatly. Still, many times this is an issue that requires lifelong management or maintenance. People and experiences can trigger the memories and the survivor needs to expect that that might happen and be prepared to cope. Above all, healing IS possible......healthy sexuality and relationships and a beautiful life are ALL possible.

"Sarah": Believe in yourself. Believe in your possibility. Believe that despite that gaping gulf in front of you, (the one that seems like it is swallowing your life whole and that you feel like you are going to be sucked into), that there is the other side of that gulf. If you can find it within yourself to see that other side, and make it your goal, then getting through the rocky gulf won't be as horrible as you think. You have a means to the end, and the reward is there.

Melody Brooke: I'd tell her to never give up on happiness. I'd make sure she knows that it lies within her. The pain of what occurred is not her fault and she is precious, brilliant and a valuable gift to the world. And to do whatever it takes to heal, and discover that she is more than what she ever knew she was capable of being.

Jennifer: Take one thing at a time and don't forget the big picture. I also try to put things in perspective by telling people to imagine how big the world is as well as the universe and the expansiveness of the solar system...Now compare that to your problems. There will always be people in better and worse situations than you, so be thankful for where you are at. Your current circumstance does not define who you are.

Diana De Rosa: My experience is probably going to be different than most because I was so young when most of this happened that I don't recall ever thinking that it would hold me back. But the one thing I do know is that at a very young age I knew I wanted to travel and see the world and I also loved to dance. I achieved both of those by believing in myself and following my dreams.

Rev. Brenda Bartella Peterson: My advice would still be the same about education, therapy and religion. But I would now emphasize that it takes all three and more. I would advise women to access every means of help available to them through community and faith resources. I would advise them to deepen their spiritual journey, as much or more, through reading rather than through church, synagogue or mosque. I would emphasize the difference between doctrine, religiosity and a spiritual journey.

~~~

Hear our message, we've been there and we all know it gets better, that's why we're here and why you're reading.

Each of us wants you to fight for your life!

You're worth it.

Our Message To You

CHAPTER 9: KEYS TO LIVING A BOUND AND DETERMINED LIFE

Where do you go from here?

Our deepest fear is not that we are inadequate.
Our deepest fear is that we are powerful
beyond measure.
It is our light, not our darkness
that most frightens us.
We ask ourselves, Who am I to be brilliant,
gorgeous, talented, fabulous?
Actually, who are you not to be?
You are a child of God.
Your playing small does not serve the world.
There is nothing enlightened about shrinking
so that other people won't feel insecure around
you. We are all meant to shine, as children do.
We were born to make manifest
the glory of God that is within us.
It's not just in some of us; it's in everyone.
And as we let our own light shine,
we unconsciously give other people
permission to do the same.
As we are liberated from our own fear,
our presence automatically liberates others.
Marianne Williamson

Keys to Living a Bound and Determined Life

You have just journeyed through the gardens of women's souls...gardens that were born full of hope and promise and then hardened by life and neglect. After years of pushing forward in their lives, not only have their souls been healed, but now their lives are a gift for themselves, their families, friends, to me and now to you.

So where are you in your life?

My goal for you after reading this book is to move in a positive direction. Grab a hold of the greatness within yourself, push the limits you've set for yourself and live your dream!

You can't tell me it's impossible. You've just read a book full of what's possible...and it's possible for you too. To get started, you need to let go of whatever is holding you back, explore what is inside of you and believe your dreams for yourself.

Before we continue, there is an issue that needs to be addressed...

If you have recently been through a traumatic experience or are going through one right now...

Get help now. Please see Appendix A: Resources. There are many, many places for you to turn. Get assistance, get therapy, read books, pray, whatever you do, fight for your life and your soul to get better and live!

Tell your story until someone listens and helps you. Grab hold of one of the women's stories in this book to be your inspiration for what your life could become until you can create that reality for yourself.

Don't let your situation make you a victim for the rest of your life. We know it gets better. **We've been where you are.**

Now, let's move onward!

Maybe you've survived a trauma but don't believe that greatness is in your future. Maybe you believe that it's okay to settle for less because, well, at least life is better than it used to be...

If this book has left you with anything, let it leave you with the idea that ANYTHING is possible in your life. You are full of possibilities and potential and you need to get out of your own way.

From my own experiences and the experiences of the women in this book, I want to leave you with my 8 Keys to living a "Bound and Determined" life...

Key #1
Forgive and Accept Your Past

Whatever has happened in your life has happened. You can't run from it and as long as you continue to try, it will have a hold on you. Instead, embrace it! Acknowledge that it happened and recognize how much you have overcome in your life. You are an inspiration.

So many times, once we've reached a place that is comfortable, we stop fighting for more. We settle into a life that we understand and we don't set goals for ourselves anymore, either because we feel we don't deserve it or because we're scared.

Who says you don't deserve more? Ask yourself this question and write down the answer, "What would you do if you had the freedom to do anything in your life?"

Have you done it?

Look really hard at your answer. Envision yourself doing it. How does it make you feel inside? Now, what is keeping you from going for it? In most cases, it is your own limiting beliefs.

At one point, these beliefs may have kept you safe, but you don't need them anymore. The world is out there for you to take a hold of and make yours!

Key #2
Be Open to Accepting Help

No matter where you are in your life or where you want to go, there are people available that can help you to achieve whatever it is that you want to achieve. However, you have to be open to getting their help.

As you read in this book, that help comes in many different forms. It could come in the form of a book, a religion, a retreat, a friend, a therapist or a coach, but there's someone or something out there specifically for you. You simply have to be open to recognizing it and accepting it when it comes.

Another component to accepting help is being aware that there's a difference between "doing things right" and "doing the right thing". You have a choice every single day to "do the right thing".

Sometimes, you may be tempted to be dishonest, because you "deserve" to get something. What you deserve is to treat yourself and others with respect. By not compromising your integrity, you can look at yourself in the mirror and be proud of the face that looks back at you.

Keep your options open and accept the help that is knocking on your door. Remember, no matter who you are or what you do, there are always people standing in your shadow. Make sure that you cast a shadow that protects and nurtures. In the end, it will always come back to you.

Key #3
Recognize the Strength from Your Past

Whatever it is that you've been through, it has made you stronger. You may ask yourself, "Well, if that's true, then why do I still feel so weak?" In answer to that, let me ask you a couple of questions in return:

Are you still focused on your past and how you've been wronged?
Do you believe that you deserve less because of your past?

If you can answer yes to either of those questions, or both, then that's why you don't feel strong. Instead, take the time to look at what you've been through and recognize how far you've come.

> It's easy to forget how far you've come
> when you are looking at where you want to be.
>
> Take the time to write down how far you've come
> and recognize just how strong you are.

Here's an exercise that you can do to help you to recognize and take ownership of your personal strength. This exercise is called "Why vs. How."

In "Why vs. How", the "why" is so much more important than knowing the "how." Let me explain what I mean.

We all know "how" to do a lot of things. And don't misunderstand me, it's important to know "how" or we wouldn't get things done. However, without asking ourselves "why" we're doing something, we can end up getting little accomplished for ourselves.

Here's the exercise:

As you go throughout your day, ask yourself "why" you do what you do. When you get the answer, ask yourself if it's important...if it's moving you forward in your life. If it is, keep doing it.

If you realize that the task accomplishes nothing for the betterment of your life or the lives of those around you, ask yourself if this is a task that can be ignored or relegated to someone else.

In the end, you'll feel stronger, more empowered and in control of your life. You may even find that you have freed up some time that will allow you to do something special for yourself!

Key #4
Wage War Against Your Brain's Status Quo
(or, Sometimes the light at the end of the tunnel is a train.)

Sad, but true! Just when we think that we're moving forward and life is going to get easier, something bad happens. Then, we're surprised, shocked or furious. After all, "Haven't I already paid my dues?"

The Bad News
After experiencing trauma, we just want a break and it's difficult to accept reality. So, what's reality? While you may have had a tough life, life continues on and struggles will happen. Bad things happen to good people all of the time. You need to accept that life is full of adversity.

The Good News

Tough times don't last. And, with every tough time that you go through, you get tougher, more resilient and more capable. Once you accept that idea, you need to make a vow to yourself to never give up.

With every passing struggle, the struggle will become easier to handle. After a period of time, you will become a light to those around you. Someone needs you, too. And, you don't have to become a speaker or an author to have a positive effect on those around you. You just need to be aware and willing to help.

Key #5
Accept That There's Greatness in Your Future

While it's easy to close your mind and just exist, it's the worst thing in the world to do to yourself! There is so much to learn and embrace. Your heart and mind crave to be stretched in new directions daily and if you stop challenging yourself to learn, your heart and mind will become numb to the possibilities that surround you.

So wake up! You can find new ideas in books, religion, hobbies, sports, and by simply being with other people!

One of the best ways to begin to accept potential greatness is to surround ourselves with friends.

Understand them and embrace them.

Friends make life more interesting and the struggles in life more bearable. Spend the time to make friends and value your relationships.

For 8 years, I lived near one of my dearest friends, Karen, in San Diego, CA. When my husband and I decided to move our family to the other side of the country (North Carolina), Karen and I sadly had the "woulda, shoulda, coulda" talk with each other.

Here's how it went…
"I wish we would have spent more time with each other."
"We should have made more plans."
"I could have moved my schedule around."

I vowed to never have that speech again and as much as I valued my relationship with Karen, I now show it. And I not only show it with Karen, but I have made changes with new friends.

Another thought about friends…not every friend is going to fulfill all of your needs in a friend. I have several friends that I can call at 2am or could call me and we would take care of each other. However, each one is different.

I have one friend that is always encouraging and telling me how wonderful I am. I need her to help me to continue to feel special. I have one friend that challenges me to strive for me and push myself to only accept the best in myself. I have another that has a son a couple of years older than my children and gives me hope that my kids are going to turn out okay.

If I put them all in the same room, they would all get along, but they wouldn't necessarily become friends of each other. But that doesn't matter. What matters is that they all fill a part of my heart. Each of them fulfills different needs within me and I need all of them in order to continue to grow. They are instrumental to my future as I believe that I am for them.

The older we get, the more difficult it gets to make new friends, real friends, so when you do, embrace them. You'll be happier and I promise you, it will make a difference in your life and theirs.

Key #7

Protect your personal time – don't find time, make time!

Once, I was talking with my coach and she said, "You need to make sure that you're spending at least an hour a day by yourself, for yourself."

I responded by telling her, with quite a bit of exasperation and with all sincerity, "But, where am I supposed to find the time?!"

She looked at me with a grin and said, "You'll never 'find' time for yourself; you have to 'make' time for yourself."

Sounds simple and logical. To me, it was profound. I had been spending so much time doing what "needed" to get done, that I was leaving out what was most important...me.

If you don't take care of yourself, you will run out of energy to take care of everything else in your life. In the end, it will make you sick. You need to do whatever it takes to safeguard the time that is a must ingredient for your health and sanity. I know that's easier said than done.

Make the time to take the time to be with yourself, exercise and eat right. You'll be happier and life will seem more manageable. The obstacles that come your way will be easier to overcome and you'll be able to get through your struggle with a smile on your face.

You'll love yourself for it!

Key #8
Go make a difference and be great!

I believe that we were all born to be great! I don't mean that every single one of us is born to be famous or rich. In my opinion, being great is relative to the impact that you have on people and you don't have to be Mother Theresa to have an impact.

One of the greatest people that I know is the mother of my childhood friend that I've mentioned before, Diane.

During a time when I stopped believing in myself and felt that no one loved me, she took me on several trips with her and her daughter. We went to amusement parks, roller skating, saw movies and stayed at the beach. I believe that her love and care for me helped me to stay alive.

Years later, when I was in my mid-thirties, I visited her and through tears, told her how much her love had meant to me. She was floored. To her, she was being caring...a simple act of kindness. To me, she had been great. She had made a significant difference in my life.

Simple acts of kindness can have a greater impact than you imagine. Volunteering at a local organization that serves needs you care about can have drastic impact on people's lives and help to keep you moving in a positive direction in your own life.

Here's a recap of the keys...

Key #1 – Forgive and Accept Your Past

Key #2 – Be Open to Accepting Help

Key #3 – Recognize the Strength from Your Past

Key #4 – Wage War Against Your Brain's Status Quo

Key #5 – Accept That There's Greatness in Your Future

Key #6 - Embrace your friends...we're all we have!

Key #7 - Protect your personal time – don't find time, make time!

Key #8 - Go make a difference and be great!

The stories you have read in this book are our lives. After trial, tribulation, abuse in every form, we all fell into a pit in our lives that we didn't think we could escape. The walls seemed too high and from where we stood, we didn't see a way out. Some of us were so damaged that we didn't think we deserved a way out.

But we did deserve better and you do, too!

We hope that our stories have helped not just because we've been there, but because we've been there and have overcome. We've found success and joy in our lives. In fact, the joy is so great, that we wouldn't change a thing. In the end, we have come full circle.

If you are still in the midst of your trauma or a survivor just on the other side, we ask that you please get help. Talk to someone, get counseling, read books, find God – do it today, do it now!

You may not believe your life will ever get better. We believe it will...
as long as you keep trying.

If you've moved on with your life, but you still aren't full of the joy that life has to offer, get help! Strive for more in your life. You deserve to be full of joy. You deserve a child-like heart and you can get it back.

Open your eyes to the world of possibilities.

We did.

And you can too.

Once you move forward and become successful, it will be your turn to pay it forward. It's time to tell your story again...not from the eyes of a victim, but rather from the eyes of the victor!

Your story can inspire others to reach for their greatness.

Give hope and live well.

Deidre

Keys to Living a Bound and Determined Life

Appendix A: Resource Hotlines

The following is in no way an exhaustive list nor is it intended to contain the exact resource that you are looking for, but if you are in a crisis or have identified a need, one of these numbers may be of help to you. All of these numbers were in working order at the time of print and are listed in alphabetical order.

Abortion Information
800-772-9100

Adoptions- Rosie Adoptions - (if you are pregnant)
1-800-841-0804

AIDS National Hotline
1-800-342-2437

Al-Anon/Alateen Hotline
Hope & Help for young people who are the relatives & friends of a problem drinker.
1-800-344-2666

Alcohol/Drug Abuse Hotline
1-800-662-HELP

Be Sober Hotline
1-800-BE-SOBER

Center for the Prevention of School Violence
1-800-299-6504

Centers for Disease Control AIDS Info
1-800-342-2437

Resource Hotlines

CHADD-Children & Adults with Attention Deficit/Hyperactivity Disorder
1-800-233-4050

Child Abuse Hotline
1-800-4-A-CHILD (1-800-422-4453)

Cocaine Help Line
1-800-COCAINE (1-800-262-2463)

24 Hour Cocaine Hotline
1-800-992-9239

Domestic Violence Hotline
1-800-799-SAFE (1-800-799-7233)

Domestic Violence Hotline/Child Abuse
800-4-A-CHILD (800 422 4453)

Drug Help National Helpline
1-800-378-4435

Eating Disorders Awareness and Prevention
1-800-931-2237 (Hours: 8am-noon daily, PT)

Eating Disorders Center
1-888-236-1188

Ecstasy Addiction
1-800-468-6933

Emergency Contraception Information
1-888-NOT-2-LATE (1-888-668-2528)

Family Violence Prevention Center
1-800-313-1310

Food Addiction
1-800-841-1515

Gay, Lesbian, Bisexual, and Transgender (GLBT) Youth Support Line
800-850-8078

Gay & Transgender Hate Crime Hotline
1-800-616-HATE

Healing Woman Foundation (Abuse)
1-800-477-4111

Help Finding a Therapist
1-800-THERAPIST (1-800-843-7274)

Herpes Resource Center
1-800-230-6039

Homeless/Runaway National Runaway Hotline
800-231-6946

Incest Awareness Foundation
1-888 -547-3222

Learning Disabilities - (National Center For)
1-888-575-7373

Marijuana Anonymous
1-800-766-6779

Mental Health InfoSource
1-800-447-4474

Missing & Exploited Children Hotline
1-800-843-5678

National Adolescent Suicide Hotline
800-621-4000

National Association for Children of Alcoholics
1-888-55-4COAS (1-888-554-2627)

Resource Hotlines

National Child Abuse Hotline
1-800-422-4453

National Domestic Violence Hotline
1-800-799-SAFE (1-800-799-7233)

National Drug Abuse Hotline
1-800-662-HELP (1-800-662-4357)

National Hotline for Missing & Exploited Children
1-800-843-5678

National Inhalant Prevention Coalition
1-800-269-4327

National Institute on Drug Abuse & Alcoholism
1-888-644-6432

National Institute of Mental Health
1-888-ANXIETY (1-888-269-4389)

National Mental Health Association
1-800-969-6642

National Office of Post Abortion Trauma
1-800-593-2273

National Resource Center on Domestic Violence
1-800-537-2238

National Runaway Switchboard and Suicide Hotline
1-800-621-4000

National Suicide Prevention Lifeline
1-800-273-TALK

National STD Hotline
1-800-227-8922

National Teen Dating Abuse Help
1-866-331-9474

National Youth Crisis Hotline
1-800-448-4663

National Victim Center
1-800-FYI-CALL (1-800-394-2255)

Panic Disorder Information Hotline
800-64-PANIC

PAVE: Promoting Awareness, Victim Empowerment
1-877-399-1346

People Against Rape
1-800-877-7252

Post-Abortion Project Rachel
1-800-5WE-CARE

Resource Hotlines

Appendix B: Contributors and Their Mantras

This is an amazing collection of women. I am honored to have been given the gift of sharing their lives with you. Where applicable and appropriate, I have written the name of their website and their personal mantra along with a thought or quote that they hold dear.

Listed in alphabetical order by their first names:

Dr. Barnsley Brown
www.spirited-solutions.com
Onwards!

Rev. Brenda Bartella Peterson
www.brendabartellapeterson.com
It's never too late to be what you might have been.

Cynthia MacGregor
There is no one in the world I'd want to trade lives with.

Dana Detrick
www.seriousvanity.com
We create everything--we have this great power!

Deidre Hughey
www.deidrehughey.com
Fear is misplaced energy – don't let it stop you, instead let it propel you forward to you own personal greatness!

Contributors and Their Mantras

Diana De Rosa
www.dianaderosa.com
Be positive – always think of your glass as being half full.

Diane Lang
www.dlcounseling.com
Tell me what I'm missing in my life.

Dr. Donna Thomas-Rodgers
www.thepowerstarters.com
I can do all things through Christ who strengthens me. Philippians 4:13

Dr. Glenda Clare
www.fragilefamiliesnetwork.com
Mountain – get out of my way!

Jennifer
Life is short and time fleeting, so be quick to love and make haste to be kind.

Jillian Montes
www.sobofitness.com
I am good enough.

Katie Custer
www.chakra-girl.com
In Lak'ech (I am another yourself.)

Dr. Karen Sherman
www.drkarensherman.com
There isn't anything I can't do.

Linda Norton
www.urangatang.com
I can do all things through Christ who strengthens me.

Melody Brooke
www.melodybrooke.com
I like myself, I love myself. I am responsible for my present and my future.

Dr. Nancy Irwin
www.drnancyirwin.com
My "mantra" is more of a visual and a rhetorical question. I keep a baby picture of myself in my daily line of vision, and constantly ask her what she needs. There is no way I can look at her face and tell her she is "dirty" or "damaged" or "guilty" or "bad." This keeps me going.

Pam Lontos
www.prpr.net
Don't tell me it's impossible until after I've already done it.

Patricia Alcivar
www.patriciaalcivar.com
Face Your Fears, Live Your Dreams!

Revvell Revati
www.revvellations.com
It's not personal.

Contributors and Their Mantras

"Sarah"

A mantra I have developed for myself is this: If you are truly afraid of something, don't run away from it. Instead, turn, and run straight at it – looking it right in the eye. Once you get right up on that fear, you'll realize that it's not as big as you thought it was, and most importantly, you are no longer fearful of your fear. You've faced it, and most of the time, you are actually facing yourself, instead of a feared harm. Once you've overcome that, you are more able to handle what life throws at you.

Sherri Stanczak

sherristanczak.webs.com/

God grant me the serenity to accept the things I cannot change; courage to change the things I can; and wisdom to know the difference.

Shirley Cheng

www.ShirleyCheng.com

Dance with your heart!

Trish Lay

www.soulsatplayproductions.com

I love you, I'm sorry, please forgive me, thank you!

Ungenita Prevost

www.ungenita.com

Follow winners & you never lose. You can be inspired by many but you have to stay true to you.

Appendix C: Some Final Thoughts

The questions that I asked the women were exactly what I was looking for, but I wanted to give each of them the opportunity to share anything else that they would like.

I was so thrilled with the responses! Some women just wanted time to add a few more thoughts. Some women posed an additional question for the reader and answered it for themselves.

In any case, they wanted to share just a little bit more with me and ultimately, with you.

Enjoy the extra tidbits!

~~~

Dr. Donna Thomas-Rodgers: I spent 15 years hiding my pain from my family and friends. I don't want anyone to feel that whatever they are going through they have to endure it alone. Sharing my story has healed me in ways that I would have never known. My hair loss was killing me softly and I was too ashamed and afraid to talk to anyone about it. I missed out on some good times by hiding. I don't want anyone else to go through that.

Katie Custer (Chakra Girl): My gratitude, Deidre, for the opportunity to reflect on who I am now, to offer more gratitude for where I came from, and to gather even more excitement about where I'm going. May your life's journey fill your coffers with endless prosperity and abundance!

Some Final Thoughts

Ungenita Prevost: Do you like the person you are? I like the person I've grown to be. I consider myself a life learner so I'm certain the older I get the better I'll be which means there will be even more of me to like.

Each and every one of us has gifts and talents to soar to new heights. We must tap into our true potential. There's a difference between existing and living. In order to live your life you have to be willing to step outside of yourself and look within to discover all your talents...your true self. When you do "find" yourself you will never wake up lost. You will have all of the tools within you to make your biggest dreams come true.

Pam Lontos: I am now owner of PR/PR a public relations firm that specializes in providing publicity to authors, speakers and experts by placing them in publications such as The Wall Street Journal, Entrepreneur, USA Today, The New York Times, Real Simple, Us Weekly, and Inc., as well as various trade journals, e-zines and radio talk shows. My clients include Brian Tracy, Oscar and Emmy-nominated actress Diane Ladd, LeAnn Thieman (Chicken Soup for the Nurse's Soul, Second Dose), Jason Jennings (Less is More), and Sy Sperling, founder of Hair Club for Men.

Dr. Barnsley Brown: What special skills, qualities, and abilities do you think women possess that have enabled you to get where you are today and to envision an even more spectacular future?

My answer: We are natural communicators, relationship builders, and team supporters, all of which help us to use our strengths and combine them with the strengths of others to achieve maximum success. AND, we know how to nurture others, biologically of course, and in everything we do. We "mother" many people in our lives, helping them become successful. This is a gift that not many men have developed.

Diane Lang: I hope this book helps others and if I can help in any way let me know. Good Luck!

Shirley Cheng: "What's your ultimate secret to success in overcoming your challenges?" My ultimate secret to my successes is my deep faith in, my gratitude toward, my hope in, and my love for Jehovah God Almighty.

I've written nine books, two of which are multi-award winners (including Embrace Ultra-Ability! Wisdom, Insight & Motivation from the Blind Who Sees Far and Wide, which has won five Parent to Parent Adding Wisdom Awards), and contributed to sixteen. I design and maintain my own Web site, http://www.shirleycheng.com, where people can learn more about me and what I do, and contact me for speaking engagements and other events. After a successful eye surgery, I hope to earn multiple science doctorates from Harvard University.

Jillian Montes: I am now a dance aerobics instructor and have created a big business from it called Sobo (www.sobofitness.com).

Trish Lay: Do you believe in living within a purpose for your life? And if so, what is it? Yes. The purpose of my life is to inspire others through love, faith, integrity, and laughter. It is so important to have an idea of why you were placed on this earth. It adds meaning and a sense of belonging; even if your purpose was to bring a child into the world. Perhaps your purpose was to pull someone from a burning home or car. Perhaps your purpose was to be a loving daughter or loving wife. We all have a purpose to being here...what is yours?

Any opportunity we have to share our story with another is an opportunity to heal. From others' encounters we learn and grow. We take a piece of what they experienced and let a piece from what we experienced go. A sense of peace can come from knowing there are individuals of like mind out there understanding similar situations. Thank you for letting me participate.

Dr. Karen Sherman: Believe in yourself – everything you need is right within you!

Some Final Thoughts

"Sarah": This sounds like a great book, and I'd love to read it when it is complete. I am 41 years old and appreciate the place where you are in your life to want to write about it. Thank you.

Melody Brooke: How has this trauma affected your relationships? Because of the nature of my abuse, I didn't really trust anyone and yet didn't know I didn't trust anyone. I just developed a way of interacting with people that kept them at a distance. My walls were internal, I appeared gregarious and open but you could never really get that close.

Most people don't realize that in order to survive most trauma our psyche has to split off a part of ourselves that holds the horror of it. If we are young when this happens we might develop Dissociative Identity Disorder (Multiple Personality Disorder). These split off parts of ourselves hold pockets of feelings, memories and even personality traits associated with the trauma. These parts of ourselves hold the key to full self awareness, self love and healing.

Cynthia MacGregor: First I am grateful for all the people—from my late mother to my many friends in my adult life—who accepted me as I was. Second there is another story I want to share of my pre-diagnosis life as a teen Touretter.

I was then Jewish (I am not any longer Jewish) and was very religious. My favorite seat in temple was in the first row but, because of my tics, I relegated myself to the back of the sanctuary after a while.

One morning, though, when I was feeling better, I dared to take my old seat up front. Sue, who had a hare lip and therefore was also a social outcast, sat with me. But as is the case with Tourette's, which is exacerbated by anxiety and pressure and nervousness (though of course I didn't know any of this at the time—remember, I still had not been properly diagnosed), as I sat there, trying very hard not to tic because the whole congregation was behind me, I got progressively worse. Just before the rabbi was to deliver his sermon, the cantor got up, leaned over the pulpit and, in front of the whole congregation, asked me if I would mind moving to the back of the sanctuary.

Now, I ADORED the cantor, and I couldn't BELIEVE he would humiliate me that way. I moved (and Sue, God bless her, moved with me), and I kept my head down for the duration of the service. I couldn't face anyone! I delayed exiting the temple till everyone else had left.

As I started to walk out, I saw the bottom of a clerical robe. Looking up, I saw the cantor. "I'm sorry. The rabbi made me do it," he apologized without preamble. I sobbed in his arms for 20 minutes. I had always thought that, no matter what happened in school, at home, or anywhere else, in God's house I would be welcome even as the freak I was. Now I knew that wasn't true either. I began to drift away from religion and God after that, returning to a belief only after finding myself living next door to an anxiety attack-plagued editor and seeing God's hand in that.

Linda Norton: Most people consider me super successful. When I look back at my history...what I've accomplished in the past 30 years, it sometimes blows me away. I believe that I have lived a life worth living, and that I can look forward to an accounting of my life with the full belief that I have not squandered a single day of it, but that I have lived, and worked, and laughed, and loved, and created, and lifted, and seen things...that only I could see. And then, I made them a reality for everyone else to enjoy, too.

I have a God-given ability to know, instinctively what works in raising children. During my childhood, I actively planned what I would do with my own children.... and then I did it. I can honestly say that my children, who are young adults now, are simply awesome. I was not able to have 100% input into their lives since they unfortunately have a very abusive father; but I was able to successfully counterbalance the flaws in his parenting style. When I die and stand before God, the two great things that I will be able to offer Him as a gift for my life are my active pursuit of obedience, plus the chain of family abuse that I broke all those years ago. Knowing that gives me the greatest imaginable peace.

Some Final Thoughts

Diana De Rosa: Right now I can't think of anything. I did send you my stories and that should help as well. I did an interview as well and it is up on www.solopreneurs.com. None of my stories ever reveal the fact that I was born with a dislocated hip socket. They just talk about the rest of my life.

Thank you for being interested in my story. To me that is the greatest gift! One other thing. My motto has been to always get back to people promptly and I believe that has helped me be successful.

Rev. Brenda Bartella Peterson: I think it might be helpful to ask the women you have chosen how they defined their values and at what point in their lives they began to clarify their values. I bought into the values of the Southern Baptist church hook, line and sinker. I was in my twenties before I better clarified my values and theology for myself.

It might be helpful to teach young women at an earlier age to define their values.

I am so pleased that you are doing this book, Deidre. I would be pleased to help you in any way...even to the point of appearing with you to promote the book before or after publication.

Jennifer: Love life and Be happy.....Live life in the now as life is always now...

Appendix D: Additional Quotes

All of the quotes on the previous pages were recommended by the women highlighted in this book. However, I received so many quotes that I ran out of room!

I didn't want to leave out any of them, so this section contains all of the quotes not previously mentioned.

African Proverb: How do you eat an elephant? One bite at a time.

Author Unknown: Do what you love, love what you do and the world will come to you.

Author Unknown: Don't wait for your ship to come in. Swim out to meet it.

Author Unknown: Whether you think you can or think you can't, you're right either way.

Author Unknown: If you don't get everything you want, think of the things you don't get that you don't want.

Christopher Reeve: Nothing Is Impossible.

Dale Carnegie: Most of the important things in the world have been accomplished by people who have kept on trying when there seemed to be no hope at all.

David Neagle: If you already know everything you need to know, then why aren't you where you want to be in your life RIGHT NOW?

Dorothy Thompson: Courage, it would seem, is nothing less than the power to overcome danger, misfortune, fear, injustice, while continuing to

Additional Quotes

affirm inwardly that life with all its sorrows is good; that everything is meaningful even if in a sense beyond our understanding; and that there is always tomorrow.

Eleanor Roosevelt: No one can make you feel inferior without your consent.

Fanny Crosby: To God Be the Glory!

Horace: Seize the day! (Carpe diem)

Jewish Folklore: This, too, shall pass.

John Shedd: A ship in harbor is safe. But that is not what ships are for.

Matthew 19.36: With God, all things are possible.

Maya Angelou: Courage is the most important of all the virtues, because without courage you can't practice any other virtue consistently. You can practice any virtue erratically, but nothing consistently without courage.

Maya Angelou: I've learned that people will forget what you said, people will forget what you did, but people will never forget how you made them feel.

Maya Angelou: Someone was hurt before you; wronged before you; beaten before you; humiliated before you; raped before you; yet, someone SURVIVED.

Maya Angelou: If you don't like something, change it, if you can't change it, change your attitude.

Maya Angelou: We make family as we make friends.

Philippians 4:13: I can do all things through Christ who strengthens me.

Reinhold Niebuhr: God grant me the serenity to accept the things I cannot change; courage to change the things I can; and wisdom to know the difference.

Scott DeMoulin: The past is history. The future's a mystery. But "now" is a gift; that's why it's called the present.

Shakespeare: To thine own self be true!

W. Somerset Maughan: It's a funny thing about life: If you refuse to accept anything but the best you very often get it.

Virginia Satir: I am Me. In all the world, there is no one else exactly like me. Everything that comes out of me is authentically mine, because I alone chose it — I own everything about me: my body, my feelings, my mouth, my voice, all my actions, whether they be to others or myself. I own my fantasies, my dreams, my hopes, my fears. I own my triumphs and successes, all my failures and mistakes. Because I own all of me, I can become intimately acquainted with me. By so doing, I can love me and be friendly with all my parts. I know there are aspects about myself that puzzle me, and other aspects that I do not know — but as long as I am friendly and loving to myself, I can courageously and hopefully look for solutions to the puzzles and ways to find out more about me. However I look and sound, whatever I say and do, and whatever I think and feel at a given moment in time is authentically me. If later some parts of how I looked, sounded, thought, and felt turn out to be unfitting, I can discard that which is unfitting, keep the rest, and invent something new for that which I discarded. I can see, hear, feel, think, say, and do. I have the tools to survive, to be close to others, to be productive, and to make sense and order out of the world of people and things outside of me. I own me, and therefore, I can engineer me. I am me, and I am Okay.